Also by Ranulph Fiennes

A Talent for Trouble
Ice Fall in Norway
The Headless Valley
Where Soldiers Fear to Tread
Hell on Ice
To the Ends of the Earth
Bothie, the Polar Dog (with Virginia Fiennes)
Living Dangerously
The Feather Men
Atlantis of the Sands
Mind Over Matter
The Sett
Fit for Life

Beyond the Limits

THE LESSONS LEARNED
FROM A LIFETIME'S ADVENTURES

RANULPH FIENNES

LITTLE, BROWN & COMPANY

A Little, Brown Book

First published in Great Britain in 2000
by Little, Brown & Company

Copyright © 2000 by Westward Ho Adventure Holidays Ltd

The moral right of the author has been asserted.

A CIP catalogue record for this book
is available from the British Library.

ISBN:
0 316 85458 1 (hardback)
0 316 85706 8 (paperback)

Designed by Andrew Barron & Collis Clements Associates
Printed and bound in Great Britain
by Butler & Tanner Ltd

Little, Brown & Company (UK)
Brettenham House, Lancaster Place
London WC2E 7EN

For Ed Victor

CONTENTS

ACKNOWLEDGEMENTS

My thanks to my wife, my mother and sisters for all the years of their support, patience and advice.

To Ginnie, Ollie, Charlie, Anton and Jill for their friendship throughout the Transglobe years and beyond.

To Mike, Ol, Flo and Mo for all the good times north and south as well as for sticking with it when things were hard.

To all my friends, co-travellers, sponsors and advisers over the years for helping in so many ways when things were going well and when they weren't.

Also, for this book, my thanks to Ed Victor, Gina Rawle, Frances Pajović, George Greenfield, Philippa Harrison and Andrew Gordon. For the photographs, my thanks to Bryn Campbell, John Clearey, George Ollen, Mike Hoover, Anton Bowring, Simon Grimes, David Mason, Mike Stroud, Morag Howell, Alan Taylor, Andy Dunsire, A. Moyes, the British Antarctic Survey, Dr Peter Duffy and Adrian Houston/*Hello!* magazine.

Ranulph Fiennes
Exmoor, 2000

**The *Benjy B*
jammed in
pack ice.
Anton Bowring,
Jim Young and
Howard Willson in
the foreground.**

'We must select the illusion which appeals
to our temperament and embrace it with passion,
if we want to be happy'

CYRIL CONNOLLY

1
GETTING STARTED

My father died of wounds in Italy in 1943, four months before I was born in Windsor, as Hitler's V2s rained down on Britain. I was proud of my heritage, and grew up keen to command the Royal Scots Greys cavalry regiment as he had. My ancestor Eustace Fiennes, from the village of Fiennes near Boulogne, had commanded William the Conqueror's troops and had personally killed King Harold of England, who, at the time, had an arrow in his eye. We Fiennes have been opportunists ever since.

When Dad joined the army in India, the Scots Greys were mounted on 600 grey horses. One of his later jobs in Palestine in 1942 was to switch his soldiers to tank warfare. A short while later they played a big part in defeating Rommel's Panzers at El Alamein. The Scots Greys learn fast.

Twenty years after Alamein I joined the Greys in Germany as an eighteen-year-old lieutenant fresh from Eton. I soon found that tank exercises, in the mud and pine forests south of Hamburg, were repetitive and uninspiring despite the menacing presence of overwhelming Soviet tank forces not far to the east. I needed something more stimulating and competitive. The regiment's colonel agreed I could start training canoeing, cross-country skiing

With Scots Greys tank and crew, 1965.

and orienteering teams to compete in army races. We won a few trophies and avoided quite a few tank exercises. I began to notice which soldiers did well, were trustworthy, excelled at twisting officers around their little fingers and could endure hardship without complaint, and which ones were liable to cause trouble.

The sad truth about peacetime tank manoeuvres was that the officers who shone more brightly were those who played by the book. There was no place for individual brilliance or initiative, largely because we were expecting and training for a short, sharp, nuclear war.

After three years I volunteered to join the SAS regiment fighting Indonesians in the Borneo jungle. On the day I received my SAS wings I became the youngest captain in the British Army, but, a few months later, I was demoted back to lieutenant and sent back to the Scots Greys. My crime was to use army plastic explosives to blow up a Twentieth Century–Fox film set in Dorset which an old friend of mine objected to environmentally. This was an initiative which neither the SAS nor the Army Board approved of, and my lifelong aspiration to command the Greys suffered a severe setback.

Back in Germany, we carried on practising endless retreats from the Soviet border. This was 1967 and, at the age of twenty-three, I felt old and as if I was getting nowhere fast. Officers who had joined the regiment two years after me were in more senior positions, which was not a good omen for my making it to CO.

Cross-country skiing, 1968; RF at right.

I was standing still but, all around me, the world was changing fast. That year a young Prince Charles went to Cambridge, there was a successful heart transplant, colour TV blossomed, the Summer of Love fluttered by, Sweden switched to driving on the right, Milton Keynes was built on 22,000 acres of virgin countryside, and Britain withdrew from Suez. The old order was disappearing fast.

A Greys captain serving in Arabia sent me a letter with a colourful stamp. 'Come and join me,' he suggested. 'No tanks, no mud and good pay.' He failed to mention that the Sultan of Oman, his boss, was involved in an escalating war with Marxist revolutionaries.

My application for the posting was approved and after a quick London course in Arabic (which I failed), I was sent to Muscat in Oman. The Sultan's senior officers included many relics of the Raj, the headquarters was a *Beau Geste*-style fortress with crenellated keeps and cannon, and our rifles were Second World War bolt-action leftovers.

I was sent south to the war zone of Dhofar and soon savoured my baptism of fire. The Marxist terrorists, at home in the jungle-clad Dhofari ravines, had received their training and automatic weapons from the Soviets. Their members far exceeded our puny Sultanate forces and they gained control of the mountains in western Dhofar during my first summer there.

There were no helicopters. The Sultan's entire air force in Dhofar consisted of two, antiquated Piston Provost fighters flown by ex-RAF pilots. Our navy was a simple, wooden dhow. Richard John, the Scots Greys officer whose letter had attracted me to Arabia, was shot through the shoulder in an ambush. His painful evacuation on the back of a mule took eight hours.

Back in Muscat I was introduced, by my new Colonel, to the reconnaissance platoon I was to lead, a rag-tag band of fifteen men and five dilapidated, open-top Land Rovers. Half the unit were volunteer Omanis; the other half, whom they hated, came from Baluchistan, a country which the Sultan had recently sold to Pakistan for £1 million.

Unlike the rest of the regiment's three infantry companies, the 'recce' platoon traditionally travelled in vehicles, so the Colonel had decided I should command it. His logic was clear: I knew how to work with tanks, so I could surely cope with Land Rovers.

The rationale of my fifteen men in having joined recce was equally straightforward. The infantry companies had no vehicles so, down in Dhofar, they would have to walk everywhere. Furthermore, the most dangerous region was the mountains, where vehicles could not travel. Recce was clearly the best choice for any sane man. The thought of entering the war zone with this motley bunch of back-seaters filled me with horror.

Major Richard John.

My recent initiation to being shot at and the sphincter-tightening experience of driving through minefields had quickly dissipated the lust for excitement which had first drawn me to Oman. I now needed a just cause to work for if I was to stick my neck out and do a good job in Dhofar. A mercenary captain, Peter Southward-Heyton, supplied me with the information needed to stiffen my spine.

'In Germany, Ran, you were a tiny cog in the vast NATO wheel, but down in Dhofar you can personally make a difference to history. I'm not exaggerating. The Soviets desperately need to control the Omani coast and thus to block 80 per cent of the free world's oil. Now they've taken Aden, Dhofar will be next. They will have a brief window of

RF with recce

platoon in Dhofar,

1968.

opportunity when this will be easy for them. This year and next. Why? Because all Oman wants freedom from the Sultan. He is undeniably reactionary. No schools, no hospitals. But soon, maybe in a year, his son Qaboos, who is half-Dhofari, will take over. He will be progressive and the people will love him. This will jerk the enemy's propaganda platform from under their feet.

'So,' he continued, 'they must move now in Dhofar. They know that. Great quantities of arms, ammunition and trained cadres are infiltrating as we speak. We will have only one infantry regiment and your mobile platoon in the whole of Dhofar. Anything you can do this year to delay the enemy's consolidation, and their preparations to expel the Sultan from Dhofar, will be vital.'

Peter died not long afterwards, but his advice gave me the boost I needed.

I blitzed the platoon, sacking the 'rotten apples' and replacing them with good soldiers I tempted away from the other three companies when their officers were away on leave. I raised the platoon strength to thirty, including five good drivers who rejuvenated our vehicles. I 'borrowed' eight extra light machine-guns, a mortar, grenades and better clothing from a friendly quartermaster. With some difficulty I formed six sections of mixed race and made a strong point of never showing favour to either Omani or Baluch.

We patrolled into little-known wadis in the Sharqeeya province, fiefdom of the Sheikh Mohammed Al Harthi, who hated the Sultan. We practised tactical vehicle movement through rough scrubland, repairing the vehicles quietly by night, and communicating via code on radios which I had also scrounged. Then I was summoned by the Colonel. News from Dhofar was all bad, including a rocket ambush that had wiped out the vehicles and many men of the recce platoon whose patrol sector I was due to take over.

'You must train your men immediately,' the Colonel told me, 'to operate on foot as well as in your Land Rovers.'

For two months, in the heat of the Omani summer, we trained on foot, by day and by night, both on the gravel plains and in the dense scrub of the Jebel Akhdar at 10,000 feet above sea level. Many of the men, exhausted, transferred back to the companies. I found replacements of a tougher disposition.

My training methods were not, so far as I knew, present in any military textbook. They stemmed from common-sense reactions to the emergency situations likely to occur in Dhofar. I remembered from SAS days that movement by night is usually preferable, silence is vital, unpredictability essential, and small units a bonus. We practised night movement and hand signals repeatedly, ambush reactions daily, and accurate shooting with live rounds weekly. I read various guerrilla warfare manuals, sent by mail order, and found Chairman Mao's advice the most sensible and easy to follow. At the end of the Omani date harvest, we took our leave of northern Oman and drove the five Land Rovers south for 500 miles.

The Rubh al Khali, or Empty Quarter, is the greatest sand desert in the world and stretches for a thousand miles from the Omani coast into Saudi Arabia. In it there is nothing permanent. The eastern fingers of the sands, through which we travelled, stretched flat and grey to the sea with a surface of black gravel and yellow pans of gypsum.

For a while we patrolled only to the north of the Qara mountains, which stretch across the length of Dhofar, separating the arid northern deserts from the fertile plain of Salalah to the south. In Salalah village the Sultan lived in a whitewashed palace overlooking the Indian Ocean.

White sand and oases of coconut palms led away west and east from the palace as far as the eye could see. The Marxist-controlled Qara mountains rose sheer from the plain only eight miles to the north of the palace. The mountains themselves, though hundreds of miles in length, were but ten miles across between southern plain and northern deserts.

Army strength in Dhofar numbered fewer than 300 men, whereas some 4,000 armed terrorists held the mountains. To drive over the only vehicle track that crossed the Qara was a lethal experience involving mines and ambush, but we were lucky. Once on Salalah plain, we began a series of ambushes, moving only by night to hide in caves and deep forest. We could usually carry enough ammunition and water for four days.

We killed many of the enemy, had many near scrapes, and lived in constant fear of mines – both the tank mines that could throw a Land Rover thirty yards and the anti-personnel devices which blew your foot through your stomach and removed your face. There were snakes everywhere. The carpet viper's venomous bite could render a strong man brain-dead in seconds. Seven-inch-long camel spiders and the even bulkier, poison-fanged wolf spiders were common.

Hyenas and wolves roamed the foothills, leopards and wild cats snarled from caves, and ticks, whose bite paralysed or poisoned, dropped on to passers-by from foliage. Twelve-inch centipedes, great scorpions and giant lizards scuttled about as we lay 'doggo' in ambush hides. A great place for a naturalist.

At night the stars were huge as we advanced in a long, silent file, sometimes with a guide, but more often using highly inaccurate maps. Patrick

**Three Omani
members of recce
platoon in
mountain ambush,
Dhofar, 1969.**

Brook, an old army friend, was ambushed in the hills one day and a bullet smashed the flask he carried on his right hip. Another drilled through his left arm. The soldiers immediately ahead of and behind him were killed. His guardian angel was on top form that day.

I always led from the front, mainly because I knew where I wanted to go and how fast a pace I needed to set. I found it impossible to convey these wishes to anyone else.

Some officers wore comfortable clothes and shaved. They stood out like sore thumbs – prime targets for enemy snipers. Nearly all my men wore standard army camouflage. I tried to dress exactly like them in order to increase my chances of survival.

In exchange for information about enemy movements, we gave food and medicine to the goat-herds in the valleys. They would ask when we would next visit so they could tell other sick people to come. Suspecting they might tell the enemy, we laid ambushes in readiness for any would-be ambushers, but sometimes we grew tired and careless. On two such occasions we nearly paid with our lives.

I learned that wherever we moved, by day or by night, I must observe every feature we passed. The sudden terror of an ambush could numb the brain. Instant reaction was crucial and possible only by knowing the whereabouts of the nearest cover – immediately.

Many of the world's greatest mountaineers have died on their way back down from hazardous ascents. Exhausted, they had dropped their guard. In Dhofar I learned never to relax within a war zone. No operation was over, no matter how successful it appeared, until every man was safely back in base.

The Voice of Cairo and Radio Aden pumped out propaganda on behalf of our enemy. Halfway through my second year in Dhofar, after a particularly vicious but successful ambush of an enemy infiltration route, my recce platoon was specifically mentioned as a Marxist target. One of our most helpful intelligence agents was murdered in his own home, in front of his parents, by a terror group led by his own brother.

Bait Kathiri desert *bedu*, Dhofar, 1970.

Our Colonel changed tactics early in 1969 as the enemy brought bigger and better weapons into Dhofar. He installed a north–south blocking line at key points across the mountains in an attempt to disrupt this lethal in-flow. My unit was to patrol the ancient Dehedoba camel trails in the rugged country immediately north of the Qara mountains and up to the Yemeni border.

For months we lived on the move in the scorching, gravel deserts, dodging enemy traps, suffering ulcerating desert sores, straying many miles over the Yemeni border and never developing a routine. The key was always to respect the enemy, but never to allow that respect to overawe and blunt the scope of our own strategy.

The fear of mines, the ever-present tension of attack or ambush, and the day-long irritations of flies and dust affected everyone. One of the companies mutinied. Their officer was a Royal Marine captain with an impatient nature. He would throw stones at soldiers lagging behind. Royal Marines may have put up with this trait, but the Arabs found it distressing. His gung-ho approach to the enemy had ended in a serious ambush and several casualties. After the mutiny he was removed and replaced by an officer more capable of compromise and subtlety.

I could sense when the recce men were on edge, though they seldom complained. The hardest times were the month of Ramadan, when no Muslim should eat or drink during daylight hours. When we needed to move fast by day, with heavy loads in the searing heat, it was doubly wearisome to fast. Since the Koran was inflexible, I decided to follow the same rules as the men. That way I could ask more from them without fear of the attitude, 'It's all right for him, he's not fasting.' Experiencing the privations of Ramadan for myself also greatly increased my already considerable respect for the innate toughness of the men, Omanis and Baluchis alike.

After Dhofar I knew never to ask for more than I was prepared to give. But, not every salutary lesson I learned from the Arabs applied equally well with European soldiers or expedition colleagues. A big bonus for officers dealing with awkward enquiries from their Muslim charges, such as the query, 'My pay will be increased next year, won't it?', was the ability to respond with a sincere '*Insh'allah*' or 'God willing', which closed the matter. This did not work with the Scots Greys.

Although I killed people in Dhofar, my conscience did not disturb me because I rarely saw the dead bodies and I knew that the individuals concerned had been trying hard to kill me. Most fire-fights took place at a distance of at least a hundred yards in thick bush or broken rock outcrops. Once, however, we killed three women in error. The fact that they were active terrorists did not soften the blow when I realised what we had done. Soon afterwards I missed the chance of bringing artillery shells down on a village sheltering a heavily armed enemy patrol because I heard children playing in the huts. My men disapproved of the missed opportunity.

Overall I was lucky that I never received orders to do anything I was morally against. I hope that I would have had the courage of my convictions if this had happened. I will never know, since the nearest I came to it was an order to sow anti-personnel mines along the Dehedoba trails which we were blocking. Innocent *bedu* sometimes used these ancient camel routes, as well as the enemy, so I hedged my bets by laying the mines as I was instructed but then placed barbed wire all around them.

Because the Sultan's army had no mines, ours were manufactured from Coca-Cola cans, torch batteries and plastic explosive. Nevertheless, they were fully capable of amputating a leg below the knee or blinding their victims with shrapnel. When I finally left Dhofar I removed each and every mine that I had laid and came within an ace of kneeling on one. A suitable epitaph would have been: 'Hoist with his own petard.'

My unofficial adviser in Oman was also one of my corporals, Mohammed Rashid. Although we met only on active duty, I knew he was

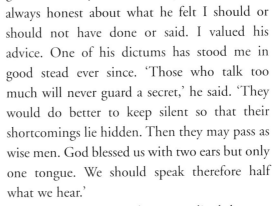

always honest about what he felt I should or should not have done or said. I valued his advice. One of his dictums has stood me in good stead ever since. 'Those who talk too much will never guard a secret,' he said. 'They would do better to keep silent so that their shortcomings lie hidden. Then they may pass as wise men. God blessed us with two ears but only one tongue. We should speak therefore half what we hear.'

Some of the victims of Dhofar.

As 1969 came to a close we realised that our blocking tactics had been only partially successful. The enemy had still managed to infiltrate huge amounts of war materials into the mountains in readiness to wipe out the Sultan's army, and soon they would be able to block the government's only resupply track over the mountains. They already controlled over 90 per cent of Dhofar. The Colonel ordered me to locate an alternate route to the western mountains, so for three months we explored the labyrinthine valleys and high, giddy ridge-lines of the gravel Nej'd region between the Qara mountains and the sands of the Empty Quarter. Eventually, we identified and then engineered a vertiginous

RF removing Mark VII anti-tank mine used by PFLOAG Marxists, Dhofar, 1970. The penknife is used to check under the mine for grenade booby-traps.

new trail which enabled the army to reach the western mountains without fear of ambush.

In October that year I was summoned by the Sultan's Intelligence Officer to penetrate deep into the eastern headquarters of the enemy and kidnap two key political commissars. The subsequent operation was the most hazardous of my army life, but, in a small way, it made up for my failure to achieve my life's dream, the command of the Royal Scots Greys.

Our ambush was eventually a success but, to avoid being shot at close range myself, I had to kill both the commissars. We removed all the documents they carried, from which Intelligence learned a great deal about the enemy's organisation. Many names and ranks of their leaders were revealed along with their intended policy.

More importantly, the death of the two commissars, in the centre of their stronghold, had far-reaching effects on the enemy morale at a key period. Tribesmen, hitherto cowed by the Marxists, fled to the government safe havens for the first time, took up arms against the Marxists and asserted themselves as anti-Communist Muslims. The enemy switched their focus to brutally suppressing defection and were wrongfooted at the crucial moment when, a few months after our operation, the Sultan was overthrown with British complicity and his progressive son Qaboos took over. It was during those key months, prior to the coup, when both Dhofar and northern Oman were ripe for revolution, that the enemy could have struck with force and sparked off a general uprising.

That they did not seize the opportunity was largely due to their uncertainty as to the mountain tribesmen's loyalty, an uncertainty first promoted by the informers who led us to kill the commissars.

Opposite: The wreck of a Land Rover blown up near the Dehedoba trails.

Right: The platoon has its bi-monthly wash at Ayun Oasis.

The day that I left the men of the recce platoon, somewhere in the wilderness of the Dehedoba trails, was one I shall never forget. I counted many of them as true friends.

Service regulations were such that I could no longer stay with the army. The problem

Recce platoon
medic giving first
aid to *bedu* on the
Salalah Plain.

went back to my inability to pass the A-level exams necessary to enter the Sandhurst Military Academy and obtain a regular commission. After eight years of service, I could sign on no more and was forced to become a civilian.

At twenty-six years of age I needed a full-time profession. The army had trained me in few skills applicable to gainful employment as a civilian, but for six months back in London I applied for a wide variety of jobs. Unemployment was then rife throughout the country and nothing came my way.

Twenty-six is quite old to start out in life with no qualifications and a lifelong ambition in ruins. I had no business connections and no sure idea of any particular career goal.

Ever since leaving school the army had provided a safety net, a great khaki umbrella which had provided my every reasonable need. Now I was on my own and, although my South African godmother had left me £8,000 in her will, I was loath to break into this nest-egg, which formed the sum total of my capital.

I spoke German, French and Arabic quite well so, perhaps, I could work in Intelligence. I applied to MI6, was interviewed and turned down. No specific reason was ever given.

My girlfriend Ginnie decided to help. We had been neighbours in Sussex since she was nine and, during my leave from Dhofar the previous year, she had helped organise a journey up the Nile, the longest river in the world, by mini-hovercraft – a project sparked off by reading Alan Moorehead's great book about that river.

On a whim, Ginnie had visited Britain's best-known literary agent for expedition writers, George Greenfield, who represented the likes of Francis Chichester, John Hunt, Edmund Hillary and Chris Bonington. Ginnie decided that I should write a book about the Nile expedition and to my great surprise and delight George took me on. Returning from Dhofar I produced the text in good time and the royalties totalled £450, which was enough to keep me going for several months so long as I lived a frugal life at my mother's house in Sussex.

Five months after leaving the army I was still receiving negative responses to all my job applications. In desperation I began to give lectures at local town halls using colour slides of the Nile expedition. Slowly I infiltrated the town-hall network and, since Britain then had an inexhaustible supply of town halls paying lecturers £18 inclusive of travel costs, I was unlikely to end up on the dole. The vast majority of my audiences were ladies of over seventy,

Overleaf: Night sentries in the Nej'd desert, 1970.

**Dinka tribal folk
at Malakal in
Sudan.**

who liked each other's company, but found it difficult to stay awake for more than fifteen minutes once the hall lights were switched off for my lecture.

The Nile expedition had gone well despite having had to plan much of it by mail from Dhofar. The resultant book had been simple to write and I had plenty of photographs for the illustrations because our cameraman had been severely burnt en route, thereby forcing me to become official photographer. Expedition lectures were easy to give so, all in all, I decided that expeditions might well provide a viable format for self-employment. If I could organise and carry out an expedition a year on a fully sponsored basis then, even though nobody would pay me for doing it, I could recoup my expenses and make a basic living while planning the next year's journey. I didn't know anybody who did this without another source of income, but there was no harm in trying.

Deciding on my first trial expedition as a civilian was helped by lessons learned from the Nile journey. The Nile is geographically remote and subject to annual floods which render impossible any travel up- or down-river over an area of Sudan far bigger than Britain. This had meant a race against the elements.

Furthermore, two major wars had been in progress in the area, with the river a main strategic feature for all sides. Israeli commandos had blown up one Nile bridge the very week we arrived in Cairo, and Sudanese rebels were regularly ambushing army troop-carriers on the Nile north of Uganda.

When my original plan to use the tracks beside the Nile in standard Land Rovers was turned down by the embassies concerned, I had decided to try the hovercraft route, since all countries through which

Hovercraft at Wadi Haifa, Nile, 1969. Charles Westmorland on the left, RF in cockpit, Nick Holder on right.

the river passes need to spray crops and stagnant water with pesticides to protect against the deadly bilharzia parasite. Spraying by hovercraft was infinitely cheaper than by air, the only alternative. I was delighted when the ploy worked and our visas were all granted. Nonetheless, for my first post-army expedition I knew I must now select a country cheap to access from London, free from wars and political strife, and not demanding a narrow time-frame of expedition activity due to seasonable limitations. Quite a tall order. Of course,

I could organise a journey up the Thames to catch some rare newt, but who would sponsor that?

Sponsorship was the key. Despite months spent wooing potential Nile sponsors by mail, that expedition ended some £5,000 in the red and, as leader, I bore the brunt of the debt. Two-thirds of my worldly wealth disappeared, but at least the journey gave me experience and a minimal platform of authority from which to launch future expeditions. I determined that from now on every expedition must be fully sponsored, down to the very last phone or fax charge and the last drawing pin. Ginnie and I also agreed we would take on no volunteer who expected any remuneration, of any sort, at any time.

Exhaustive discussions over maps at the Royal Geographical Society eventually led us to decide on an expedition to the Jostedalsbre glacier in central Norway. I called Land Rover, who had said no to sponsoring vehicles to tow our Nile hovercraft trailers the previous year. We had eventually bought second-hand Land Rovers and BBC News had shown prime-time footage of these vehicles in the Nubian Desert. So pleased were Land Rover that they now agreed to loan me three vehicles for Norway. A good start.

George Greenfield, my agent, persuaded Harold Evans, then editor of

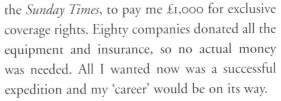

the *Sunday Times*, to pay me £1,000 for exclusive coverage rights. Eighty companies donated all the equipment and insurance, so no actual money was needed. All I wanted now was a successful expedition and my 'career' would be on its way.

'Why do you risk your life on expeditions?' I am constantly asked. The popular, romantic answer is a mixture of 'Because it's there' or 'We do it for the country . . . British explorers have always led the way,' or at least: 'I love remote places where no man has trod before.' To respond by admitting I need to make a living and that expedition-leading is my livelihood is not always

With Roger Chapman and Ginnie, a month before we were married. Newcastle quay, 1970.

appreciated. 'Surely,' the interrogation continues, 'there is an easier way to make a living?' Given my circumstances, I have to disagree. Fate, army training and a lack of A-levels led me to do what I seemed to be best at doing. Ginnie and I agreed we would aim high but start out with caution. We would eventually go for the big ones, the Everests of our chosen profession, when the time was right, but our first sortie in Norway would be less dramatic – or so we intended.◆

The Lessons Learned

Never show favour between your charges

Sack and replace earlier not later

Be observant in readiness to react

Don't relax too soon

Lead with subtlety

Don't ask your team for more than you can give

Speak half what you hear

Go for the line of least resistance

Aim high but start with caution

'Wear your learning, like your watch,
in a private pocket and do not pull it out and strike it
merely to show you have one'

CHESTERFIELD

2

THE LEARNING
PROCESS

As a teenager I spent several holidays in the Norwegian mountains and, on leave from the army, journeyed across the Jotunheim glacier region of central Norway with five friends. One of our intentions, at that time, had been to follow the course of an ancient drift trail via which, hundreds of years before, coastal herders had driven cattle and fjord-ponies, then famous all over Europe, across the great glaciers to the interior. The last of these ancient 'drifts' crossed the Jotunheim ice-fields in 1857, but by then the gently sloping edges of the glacial tongues leading up to the snow plateau had begun to melt and recede. Their slopes soon became too steep and dangerous for animals.

Our drift journey of 1967 failed due to poor equipment and the sorry lack of skiing skills of some of the team, despite the glowing reports each had given of his skiing prowess when applying to join us. I made a mental note to personally check out people's professed skills in future and never again to take CV propaganda on trust.

In 1970 I decided to use that early failed journey as a basis from which to fashion my first 'professional' expedition. Setting a precedent, which I was to follow religiously for the next three decades, I approached my literary agent

Roger Chapman conducting a survey in Norway, 1970.

with my draft plan before wasting a moment, or spending a penny, on organisation. George looked carefully at my outline Norway plans and gave them an immediate thumbs-up. He was confident he could sign up John Anstey, the *Daily Telegraph*'s magazine editor, and the ITN boss, Don Horobin, to cover the story.

With George's letter confirming this, I was able to approach sponsors with confidence since they could be sure of getting value for money in terms of publicity. Without such proof of media coverage, I knew to my cost that meaningful sponsorship would never be forthcoming.

The Norway prospectus, which George had passed to his influential editor friends, was simple but bubbling with action and would clearly make for good photographs and film at a reasonable cost. The aim was not merely to ski over the high glacial drift route but, at the behest of the Norwegian Hydrological Department, to accurately survey the Fabergstolsbre glacier. The director in Oslo stressed that this survey would be of 'extreme topical interest'.

These two activities might not in themselves have sparked the interest of ITN. The icing on the cake to them was the novel way by which we would access the glacier and, later, descend from the ice-fields back to our fjord-land base: once established in fjord-land, we would charter a suitable aeroplane to fly us over the ice plateau and drop us by parachute, together with all the delicate survey gear, on to the exact spot from which our glacial survey could best be executed. This would save many days hauling heavy equipment and survival gear 6,000 feet up steep and hazardous ravines.

Once the survey work was done, we would follow a drift route west for two days over the ice-fields, hauling the sponsored equipment on sledges, and descend to the nearest roadhead in the valleys far below by way of the Briksdalsbre glacier and river. Our parachuted equipment would include rope and inflatable boats. The whole expedition would take less than a month to complete and, if it worked, would serve as a blueprint for the future.

In the British Army I had never started on a new job without a period of apprenticeship but, in Dhofar, new officers were often let loose in the war zone as greenhorns. This resulted in many deaths, when costly lessons learned by one unit were not passed on to the troops taking over the job. To avoid this sort of folly I determined to take advice from the best in the expedition business. But how to find these experts? The *Yellow Pages* were not helpful in terms of Expedition Advisers.

In the twenty-first century things have changed enormously, and you can access instant advice, even detailed maps of Norwegian glaciers or remote Brazilian streams, on the Internet. Or you can visit the Expedition Advisory Office of the Royal Geographical Society in London and use their computers to study the most recent, detailed reports of previous expeditions to just about every remote spot in the world.

Back in 1970 the sources were fewer, but the UK's expedition supremo was an army major, John Blashford-Snell of the Royal Engineers. John was the founder of the Scientific Exploration Society, of which I was an early member. I called him and he agreed to help out.

He studied my plans, gave helpful criticism, loaned me a good deal of specialist equipment and showed me lists of individuals with skills and experience. All were summarised character-wise, so I could judge, for instance, whether my need for a surveyor with parachuting skills was dire enough to put up with an irascible egomaniac. In this and many other ways John helped to get me going. Today, remembering his early support, I try to help aspiring expeditionists either with advice or by passing them on to contacts with the relevant knowledge.

In Norway I needed a team of sixteen fit people with specialist abilities, including parachuting, whitewater-rafting and mountaineering skills. Some should also be familiar with field survey work, and the overall group must include research students, scientists, a doctor, and three off-road vehicle driver-mechanics.

Starting as I meant to continue, I told all the applicants that none would receive any remuneration or expenses; that they would need to sign a contract not to write books or give lectures for one year after the journey's conclusion; that they must fully insure themselves and their belongings; and that they must agree to my leadership. This meant they must accept up front that they might be kicked out at any time, in which case they would need to pay their way back home. Lastly, they could not keep any sponsored item, even underpants, when the expedition was over.

If they did not like this, then there was no need for them to sign on in the first place. None of this seemed to deter any of the applicants, whether they had responded to word-of-mouth advertising in ex-army and university circles or whether I had telephoned them out of the blue on John's advice.

Some came because they had a specific research interest, for example a British Antarctic Survey glaciologist and a student zoologist keen to discover new microscopic 'worms' on the glaciers. An important addition to the team was ex-army captain Roger Chapman, who had received an MBE for bravery on a recent Blue Nile expedition. A whitewater expert, Roger was studying geography at Oxford University. He was also a qualified surveyor, a langlauf skier and a keen parachutist.

I delegated all survey matters to Roger, and the parachute planning to Don Hughes, chief instructor of the Netheravon Parachute School. Don soon established that my previous assumption that we could jump on to the glacier at any time in summer was quite wrong. Roger discovered, likewise, that glacier survey work was a bad idea outside the middle two weeks of August. Suddenly a tight time structure was imposed on the project and our preparations had to speed up.

I soon learned that many of the team had been economical with the truth when completing the initial skills questionnaire I had sent them, so I instituted crash training programmes in parachuting, surveying and whitewater work. There was no time for mountaineering.

On 11 August 1970, thirteen men, three women and three Land Rovers took a ferry to Norway. On board Don queried my carefully planned schedule.

'You say we will jump in two days' time,' Don challenged, 'but today's forecast predicts high winds and low cloud. The Jotunheim area has the highest rainfall in Europe and the glacier spends three-quarters of any year swathed in local mists – never mind the cloudbase. What happens if we get

nil visibility above the glacier for the next week or so? You must be ready to postpone the survey programme because I am definitely not letting anyone jump in bad conditions. Even if you were SAS freefall experts I'd say the same thing. But you lot are decidedly unexpert.'

I was equally adamant. 'We can't postpone the survey for more than three days. We only have the full survey team until the end of the month, and they can't work on misty days. With no triangulation point sightings, they can't even start work.'

The argument went back and forth, so we agreed to compromise and hope for the best. My budget allowed for only a single day's charter so we must be sure of fine weather before calling the aeroplane up from Bergen.

On 13 August the weather looked good so I took the plunge. When the Cessna seaplane reached our base beside Lake Loen, I could see it

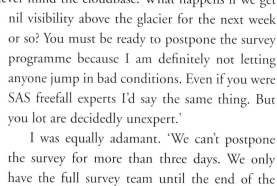

En route to the glacier jump. L to R: Patrick Brook, Bob Powell, David Murray-Wells, Roger Chapman, RF.

was not the model that I had asked for or expected. It was, however, the only plane available which could feasibly do the job. We would take off from the lake in two groups of six, fly to 10,000 feet and then jump, on Don's prompting.

Since all the previous training back in Netheravon had involved jumping from a spacious Rapide with wheels, whereas this cramped Cessna had metal floats with large rudders, we all needed to retrain at the last minute. Don handled this on the wooden jetty to which the Cessna was lashed. One by one he had us reach out of the little cabin door to grasp a narrow wing strut. Then followed a clumsy lurch from the doorway to reach the float below with both feet. Even with no 120mph slipstream this was far from easy.

To simply let go of the wing strut in this position would be very dangerous, as our bodies would almost certainly blow back into the steel float rudders. So, Don explained, to avoid decapitation, we must jump sideways and outwards just before relaxing our grip on the strut.

I would be first to jump and did not relish the idea. I glanced at the others. They all looked unconcerned, but I knew this must be an act; they were just as petrified as I was.

The *Sunday Times* photographer had hired a helicopter to record the jump. Next day the paper would show a photo of Roger dropping towards a dizzy void edged by sharp, black crags and serried ranks of crevasses far below. The banner headline blazed: 'THE WORLD'S TOUGHEST JUMP'.

I did not fancy landing in a crevasse or being battered by thermals against the 6,000-foot cliffs which fell away on two sides of our tiny target snowfield. I tried to remember how to fall for fifteen seconds in a perfect star shape, how to pull the chute release handle while remaining stable and how to steer the chute to a safe landing.

I had learned the secret of dealing with fear in Dhofar. Keep a ruthlessly tight clamp on your imagination. With fear, you must prevent, not cure. Fear must not be let in in the first place. Think of anything but the subject of your fear. Never look at the void you are about to jump into. If you are in a canoe, never listen to the roar of the rapid before you let go of the riverbank. Just do it! Keep your eyes closed and let go. If the fear then rushes at you, it will not be able to get a grip, because your mind will by then be focusing on the technical matter of survival.

That jump was memorable. I hit one hand hard against the float and cartwheeled out of control into space. I narrowly avoided missing the drop zone altogether, but luck was with me and, like most of the others, I made a safe landing. The last man to drop was dragged by surface winds to within

twenty-five yards of the cliff edge and bruised his ribs. Most of the equipment chutes were retrieved and we camped as night fell.

The next day we hauled the heavy gear on sledges between the crevasse fields, and established a camp of three two-man tents at the upper reaches of the Faberg glacier. Eight days remained to survey this formidable, frozen river plunging steeply down its captor ravine to the lush valleys below.

Three teams with sledges and theodolites set out in different directions to establish high control points. I left them to make my own way to our Land Rover camp 3,000 feet below. Later that day I toiled back up with a rucksack of fresh radio batteries but found, at the level of the snowfields, that the temperature had risen to just above freezing and the glacier was lashed by driving sleet – ideal conditions for hypothermia. After an anxious hour plodding upwards in the dark, deafened by the roaring deluge of melt-water pouring down from the upper glacier, I located the tents but nobody answered my calls. To my considerable alarm the tents were all on their sides in pools of melt-water. Worse still, equipment, including sleeping bags and clothing, was scattered about in sodden heaps. The survey groups had spent the day working on separate high features over six kilometres away. When they left the camp that morning the sun had shone in a cloudless sky, but they were all experienced in mountain safety, so how could they have failed to take even their sleeping bags? For hours I called out and shone my torch into the thick mist which now covered the crevasse fields, but nobody came back.

Opposite: Roger Chapman falls towards the tiny drop-zone between crevasse fields and cliffs.

Right: Peter Booth tries to steer away from a giant crevasse.

Roger, a man of wide expedition experience, wrote in his diary of his troubles that night. 'We slithered and fell on the ice, sometimes disappearing up to our thighs in glacial streams. Without crampons it was not easy, but we dared not rope up for, if one of us fell, we would all have slid over the top . . . Because our loads were so heavy that morning we had dispensed with both tent and sleeping bags. How stupid we were!'

They finally found the camp, where I gave them some brandy. Shivering uncontrollably they stripped naked. The sleeping bags were still sodden so two climbed into each bag to share body heat. Somehow everybody made it back to camp and the survey work was completed on time in between storms and low cloudbanks.

That was the last time I trusted anyone, no matter how brilliant their reputation, to take care of their own safety. I realised that, if the survey groups had come to grief, I would have been blamed. Thereafter I risked causing irritation and indignation by checking and double-checking safety measures, be they spare radio batteries or merely lifejacket whistles, whenever applicable.

Once the survey was done, the paperwork was sent down to the valley base camp with the glaciologist and the zoologist. Six of us, including our Swedish doctor, Henrik, remained on the icefield awaiting the two top Jotunheim guides, who were to lead us some forty kilometres east over to the old drift trail to our chosen descent route, the Briksdal glacier.

I had chosen the Briksdal because it was far steeper than the other twenty-seven glaciers that descend from the Jostedal ice plateau, and only by descending a steep ice incline could we hope to rope the heavy, laden sledges down to the river below. Gentler glaciers, split by crevasses, would prove insuperable obstacles. Such was my theory, anyway. To find the upper icefalls of the Briksdal the guides were essential, so I was relieved when they turned up. Tough and weather-beaten, they knew more about the ice-fields than anyone alive. David, the elder man, had lived up there at the start of the war, when the only parachutists likely to drop in were Nazis.

Neither man spoke English, but Henrik translated. His words were a shock. 'They advise us not to proceed with the Briksdal descent, because of the weather and dangerous crevasses.'

I argued with them, to no avail. Henrik was a man of huge experience. He was also our only ice climber of any note. He said, 'I agree with the Norwegians. I have climbed ice and rock in the Alps, Lapland, Africa and the Himalayas. There are four reasons we should not attempt this. We are now in the period of maximum melt, so there will be avalanches. We have no suit-

Crossing from the
drop zone to the
survey camp.
L to R: Roger
Chapman,
Peter Booth and
Bob Powell.

Above: Peter Booth
and Bob Powell
with survey
poles on the
Fabergstolsbre.

Overleaf: Geoff
Holder and Bob
Powell during the
descent of the
Briksdalsbre.

**Bob Powell,
Roger Chapman
and Geoff Holder
above the final
icefall of the
Briksdalsbre.**

able ice-climbing gear. None of you has previous ice-climbing experience. Lastly, the guides know best.'

The guides then added a new horror story, which Henrik translated.

'Jan says, on the Briksdal, this mist and rain will dislodge tons of falling ice all day. He says you must now abandon your heavy duty gear here and go down by the easier Faberg glacier. David says that there are icefalls on the Briksdal which even he has never climbed – in fact, he doesn't know anybody who has.'

Realising I was beaten and sensing that Henrik's words would soon infect the others' morale, I moved from the attack to the compromise. I was lucky, for the guides wanted to be as helpful as they felt the circumstances allowed. They finally agreed to guide us two-thirds of the way to the Briksdal and then leave by way of another glacier with any of us who wished to follow their advice. In the event only Henrik left the team, probably because only he truly appreciated the nature of the dangers ahead.

We spent three days and nights descending the icefalls of the Briksdalsbre, an unforgettable and nightmarish experience, during which we lost much of our sponsored equipment down crevasses. Halfway down, I made radio contact with Henrik and our Land Rovers. They and some sixty members of the Scandinavian and UK press were scanning the icefalls with binoculars from the valley below.

'You must go back, Ran,' Henrik advised. 'Five days ago a team of Norway's top glacier climbers tried to complete the first ascent of the Briksdal with the best equipment. They failed when their leader was hurt. They say descending is even more dangerous than going up, as you can't see or plan a safe route. Avalanches fall everywhere.'

I would have followed Henrik's advice but, since we were already about halfway down, it seemed less dangerous to try to continue. We already knew about the avalanches, huge masses of ice chunks cascading down the face of the icefalls. So, we continued with the descent and by great good luck we finally escaped with bloody hands, bruised ribs and our lives. Arriving at the glacier's snout we inflated our remaining rubber boats and careered down the Briksdalsbre river to the roadhead below. The Scandinavian media, who had been predicting our demise for several months, were suitably impressed by our survival, as were our sponsors, and I was ready to move on to a more ambitious expedition: marrying Ginnie two weeks after our return to Britain.

Together we plotted our next move. Writing a book about the Norway experience, we lived in a bothie in Wester Ross, where Ginnie had once worked for the Scottish National Trust. We ran low on funds and could not afford to drive south to London when we needed research maps. Luckily, the makers of the James Bond films were at the time searching for a new Bond, and Cubby Broccoli, the producer, decided to find an 'English gentleman type'. For some reason the agency decided I might fit the bill and paid for my return ticket to London. I failed the interviews but, by fortuitously bumping into the Scots Greys' Colonel in Whitehall, picked up an offer to lead an army expedition in Canada. One of the Greys captains had recently proposed a river journey in the Yukon, but the relevant Canadian authorities had turned him down. In its place they mentioned that, in 1971, the province of British Columbia was to celebrate the centenary of its formation as an independent territory. 'We would value a venture from the old country,' they suggested, 'to commemorate the remarkable river journeys of the mostly Scots pioneers who opened up British Columbia in the first place.'

The Scots Greys, overworked with the Irish troubles, had few men to spare, but I was still on the regimental reserve so the Colonel decided I would be ideal for the job.

'If you agree,' he encouraged, 'I will let you have two or three men and some supplies.'

In Edinburgh I chose three Scots Greys soldiers with whom I had worked in Germany. One was a mechanic and all were fit.

Ginnie spent two months in the archives and map room of the Royal Geographical Society. She found a route, by way of nine different rivers, which might take us on an unprecedented 3,000-mile journey, entirely by boat, from the Yukon down the length of British Columbia to the American border. The British Army and the government of British Columbia wholly approved of the project.

Having run out of money, I took a job in London as an actor with the

Geoff Holder and Roger Chapman try to stop RF's boat just above the Briksdalselve waterfall. With RF on the upturned boat is Peter Booth.

BBC's *World About Us* series. My co-star was a Cockney actress, Liz Fraser, who, like her colleague Barbara Windsor, had come to fame in the *Carry On* films. Much of the filming in early 1981 took place in the London sewers and, during long waits for the highly unionised film crews, I managed to organise the Canadian expedition.

The BBC agreed to film the journey and the *Observer* said they would send a photographer, so the obtaining of sponsors became a great deal easier.

Although the five-month journey in British Columbia would be entirely by river, I was worried that there were areas the size of Wales with no access roads. Fuel, for the outboard engines of our rubber boats, would only be able to reach us via remote forestry tracks. Ginnie agreed to drive a vehicle to deliver the petrol and oil, and the Scots Greys lent us a BER Land Rover. I later discovered that BER stands for Beyond Economic Repair. 'But don't you worry,' the Scots Greys quartermaster assured me, 'it may be usable with great care.'

The Nile journey had taught me never to assume unmitigated heat in hot countries, nor extreme cold in polar zones. We had set out for Egypt and the Sudan with cotton clothes and sun hats, but, for the first few days, experienced only snow and ice. This time we packed both hot- and cold-weather clothing.

The army loaned me an office desk in Whitehall as soon as I had completed the BBC work in the sewers. I was seated directly opposite the Director of Army PR, who was of the opinion that soldiers going on expeditions of the type I was planning was the best possible publicity for peace-time military personnel. Sadly, this was the only time in my life that I met up with this healthy attitude in such a key position.

I remembered that when our hovercraft expedition had finally reached Cairo, the then British ambassador had given me a message from the Ministry of Defence in London with orders that the expedi-

Left: Joe Skibinski, Jack McConnell and RF in Wales, training for the Canada expedition.

Opposite: Ginnie and RF in Fort Nelson, with (L to R) Stanley Cribbett, Ben Usher, Richard Robinson and Paul Berriff.

tion be cancelled and that under no circumstances should we leave the UK. This message had been addressed to my home and arrived a day late, so my mother had sent it on to my first forwarding address, the Cairo embassy. Since then, I have never taken 'No' for an answer merely because the negative party is some apparently all-powerful authority. The key to removing bureaucratic obstacles is to identify the person, not just the department, concerned and then deal with him or her face-to-face.

The soldiers came south and we trained in Wales and on the Thames by Battersea Bridge. Of course, I would have preferred a river more relevant to the thundering rapids of British Columbia, but the secret to the financial viability of expeditions is never to get in the red. You have to make do. I found sponsors for one twelve-foot and two sixteen-foot inflatable boats. The soldiers stayed in a London army barracks, which lent them transport, and I continued to work in the Ministry in between boat trials. By then Ginnie and I were proud owners of a basement flat close by Earls Court tube station. Ginnie completed the detailed route planning for Canada and joined us on our Thames outings.

We soon learned that the critical factor when planning rubber boat travel is the hump. The heavier the boat the greater the engine power needed to push the hull up on to the water's surface, so that the drag factor is minimised and the boat can skim along, 'off the hump', using minimal fuel for maximum distance.

By careful estimation of which river in Canada would flow at what speed, we could make a stab at how much fuel we must carry between the often distant resupply points. The fuel supply, if excessive, would soon make our boats too heavy to skim, or get 'off the hump', in which case fuel consumption per mile would more than double. The problem was complex, but we had to get it right.

Answers to Ginnie's enquiries about different river conditions came slowly from outstations in Canada, often doom-laden and nearly always based on hearsay. Yes, the writer had indeed spent forty years living beside the canyon, but no, he had never actually taken a boat down there, nor did he know of anybody that had been damn fool enough to do so, apart from two drunkards in a stolen boat who were never seen again. This sort of reply, and it was fairly typical, did not help our planning.

The RAF flew us to Alberta late in June, and we drove north for three days up the Alaska highway. The BER Land Rover leaked like a sieve in the frequent rainstorms and its battery oozed acid fumes into the cramped cab.

Before undertaking the main north–south river expedition, I wanted to

Stanley Cribbett and RF fighting the power of the Nahanni.

**Two of our three
boats finally reach
the Virginia Falls.**

work the men and boats in really rough water. The Nahanni, in the North-West Territories, is famed as Canada's fastest river. If we could travel upstream some 500 miles to Fort Nelson, to the Nahanni's Virginia Falls, twice the height of Niagara, we should stand a fair chance of success on tackling the turbulent rivers of British Columbia.

The Nahanni journey proved an excellent shake-out. The soldiers were tough and resourceful, the BBC film team were a pain in the neck, and Bryn Campbell, the *Observer* photographer, a positive asset. Ginnie, based in Fort Nelson, manned a field radio and kept in touch whenever conditions allowed. The rapids were wicked and the river's speed awesome. Many times we were unable to push upstream against the sheer weight of water, but, on each such occasion, patience and lateral thinking produced an answer.

By the time we had reached the Falls and negotiated the hazardous return journey to Fort Nelson, through one of the biggest forest fires in local memory, we had learned a lot about each other.

On most expeditions under pressure, a 'them and us' attitude will develop, giving all parties somebody to complain about. This can be destructive if it lowers the ability of the team to progress. But, from a television film director's point of view, such stresses and strains can make wonderful view-ing.

I had once watched a TV film of sailor John Ridgway taking a cramped yacht crew around the world. A two-man film crew had stirred up resentment on board expressly, it seemed, to highlight antagonisms and spice up their film. I was aware that the BBC might try this in Canada, and the warning signs were not slow in surfacing.

On the Nile journey, our photographer had suffered severe burns to both hands when pouring petrol into a can filled with sand. Twenty yards away and down-wind, another team member, on the other side of a Land Rover, had lit a cigarette and . . . *boom* – one burnt photographer.

Ben Usher and the BBC boat on the Fraser river.

Ever since that incident, I have always insisted that nobody ever pours petrol, even if they think they are alone, without first screaming the word

'*Petrol!*' as a warning. In Canada the BBC crew found this safety procedure odd, indeed undignified, and ignored my ruling. The soldiers took note.

One of the BBC crew, their helmsman, loved cigars and lit up whenever he felt like it. We often needed to fill the boats' fuel tanks with petrol in midstream for, in the canyons, there was nowhere to stop. I therefore banned all smoking on board, although two of the soldiers were heavy smokers. They understood the sense of this, but expected me to apply the same rule to the BBC.

When polite no-smoking requests to the BBC helmsman were ignored, I lost my cool and threatened him with dismissal next time we touched civilisation. This mini-confrontation was gleefully recorded on film and my relations with the film crew went downhill from then on over the next three, high-pressure months. Slowly, and subtly, they began to subvert the soldiers.

Unavoidable and ongoing discomfort, fear of ever bigger rapids ahead and lack of funds for any amenities when we came exhausted to rare, riverside villages began to erode the soldiers' loyalty to me. I was aware of this, but could do little to prevent it.

I well remember a day of forked lightning and impressive whirlpools, when we were all tense with apprehension. A first attempt to ram the boats upstream through a formidable series of rapids had failed. I knew we must deflate the smaller boat and carry it through forests, but the TV crew were against it and the soldiers conducted a silent mutiny of inaction. Darkness was nigh, and non-stop rain would swell the river overnight, so there was no time for patient discussion. I began to deflate the small boat myself and one by one the soldiers joined me to help.

In an action situation, I believe, there is no better way out of many deadlocks than for the leader to get on with the job himself (or herself) and, where feasible, simply to ignore the arguments and inactivity of the dissenting parties. Sometimes it is clearly best for an expedition leader to lay down the law and then stick to it through thick and thin, ignoring any muttering in the ranks. But, so long as it does not endanger life or the long-term aims of the expedition, a middle course of diplomatic appeasement is more useful. The skill of the leader is in knowing when to choose which tactic. Be flexible most of the time, but remember that one option is to be inflexible some of the time.

A week after we crossed the Yukon border and followed the Hiland river

Jack McConnell in the Rocky Mountains.

Each boat could
carry 500lb and
three men. Often
we were thrown
high in the air or
sucked down into
whirling rapids.

'The thing is so difficult it is not worth attempting.
The thing is so difficult I cannot help attempting it'

ANDRÉ

3

MAKE OR BREAK

If the Norwegian expedition had been a good launch point into the specialist world of expeditions, the British Columbia journey served as a step up the ladder. Its success opened doors to sponsors and gave us confidence that, as a married couple, we could make a dependable living from running expeditions.

We could have moved on to another river journey or switched back to hovercraft or parachutes. There were dozens of permutations, but they were not quite what we needed now. There was surely a higher level of attainment. A journey of true exploration in a land where no man had ever been. A geographical goal not as yet reached.

Hillary and Tensing had ascended Mount Everest and Chichester had sailed solo around the world. They had been the first to do so. Many thousands of others would later follow in their footsteps, but merely as also-rans. Priority was the key. To be second was of no value to us, since it would not warrant sponsorship.

Ginnie was adamant. To be successful in our chosen line of business we must never waste time in planning expeditions which somebody, anybody, had ever done before. We must be the first humans, not merely the first

Amphibious
vehicle trials off
North Greenland.
Geoff Newman in
the cab.

British, to 'get there'. Such a policy would mean, of course, our failure rate would be high: to believe otherwise would be unrealistic and conceited.

I could think of many individuals who had achieved what we were after – explorers who discovered and mapped new territory or travelled where no man had been before. Cook, Columbus and Livingstone were obvious examples, as was, much more recently, Wilfred Thesiger in Arabia.

But time was running out. Within three or four years, high-orbiting satellites would scan and map the last hidden jungles and ice-caps. We might, in the 1970s, still be just in time if we put our skates on. We might still go where no human had trod.

'Why not,' Ginnie suggested one day, 'circumnavigate the world, not the easy way, but along a line of longitude passing through both Poles?'

I checked out the idea on a six-inch globe and, using reference books, confirmed that nobody had yet done such a journey. We would need an icebreaker, a resupply ski-plane and some £29 million worth of sponsorship to stand the remotest chance of success. At that time we had £210 in the bank, owned a very second-hand Mini van, a Jack Russell terrier and a heavily mortgaged, semi-detached house near Hammersmith Bridge. Our sole income came from my infrequent pay cheques from the Territorial Army.

Nonetheless, if we were to progress from the ongoing mediocrity of run-of-the-mill expeditions to truly innovative projects, we must go soon for a make-or-break challenge. The Transglobe expedition was therefore launched on paper in early 1973, and was to involve both of us full-time for the next ten years. Over that period we descended to and hovered around the breadline, for all our energies were focused on the venture, leaving minimal time to earn a living.

At the beginning we decided that we would retain sole leadership of the project and we would never pay anybody anything at any time. Even the smallest item must be sponsored. To ensure this dictum was never transgressed, we opened neither bank account nor credit facility.

We needed – at no cost – an office, a phone and a large, storage facility in central London, so I approached my Territorial SAS Regiment's colonel.

Would the SAS sponsor the expedition? Would they give us an office and store at their barracks near Sloane Square? Because of my indiscretions with explosives six years before, the SAS boss, Peter de la Billière, agreed to the sponsorship only on the condition that the SAS colonel who had sacked me from the regular SAS now become the official overseer of the Transglobe project. This was agreed and we at once began working from an attic office in the barracks.

The meticulous polar research work, mostly in London and Cambridge, took me a year. The only feasible route, it transpired, was to follow as closely as possible the longitudinal line 0°/180°, known as the Greenwich Meridian. From Greenwich we would travel south through Europe and Africa to Antarctica. After crossing Antarctica via the South Pole, the route headed north up the Pacific past Fiji to Canada's west coast. When ice in the Bering Straits blocked the way, we would jink east up the Yukon and Mackenzie rivers, through the North-West Passage, and over the Arctic Ocean via the North Pole. Thence, back down to Greenwich.

At four critical places around the globe we would only be able to progress if we reached them during a short polar time window. If we missed any one of these slots, due to any kind of delay, we would simply have to wait there for twelve months.

If all went well everywhere and there were no such delays, we might be able to complete the journey in just over three years. I based all my plans on bad weather conditions.

We approached over 3,000 companies during the first two years in London. Seven hundred and sixty of them had agreed, by 1975, to provide us with their goods or services. To persuade the reluctant hard-headed business-men to give us many millions of pounds' worth of support for a project, which looked nigh-on impossible, required the basic arts of the salesman. These arts I rapidly acquired. Although I did not tell outright lies, I learned to use the English language in a directional manner. An example of this specialised skill is worth giving.

My literary agent arranged a meeting with editor Donald Trelford and the owners of the *Observer* in order to persuade them to pay us £25,000 for exclusive rights. I made the expedition sound as exciting and risky as possible. The following day, I lunched with a group of top insurance brokers to encourage them to fully insure the entire expedition free of charge. I assured them that the expedition was planned in such a way as to avoid all risks: the journey would be about as 'exciting as a Tupperware tea party'.

Thanks to the elasticity of the English language, we gained both the *Observer* contract and the free insurance cover.

After five years' full-time work, we obtained the full £29 million of hard-ware, including such items as a 42-year-old ice-strengthened ship, a resupply ski-plane and £2 million worth of fuel delivered to various remote points around the world.

The biggest obstacle by far, and one which did often seem insuperable, was bureaucracy. The Foreign Office had never given any private expedition their blessing to go to Antarctica. Only government-approved operations had ever been there, since, without assistance with fuel for resupply, no Pole journey would be feasible. Only the United States South Pole Authority could grant this and, without an official request from the Foreign Office, they would never do so. The Foreign Office would not move a muscle without the blessing of the Royal Society. The Royal Society would not consider us without the prior approval of our plans by the British Antarctic Survey.

Private British expeditions wanting to go to Antarctica were naturally anathema to the British Antarctic Survey. They considered the frozen continent to be their territory and did their level best to preserve it from all irresponsible (meaning non-British Antarctic Survey) outsiders. To date, they had a 100 per cent success rate.

For four years, despite maintaining an almost constant stream of requests, I was steadfastly turned down. Antarctica was a no-go area and would remain so unless I could somehow break through the rock-steady bureaucratic defences.

I fared no better in terms of the Arctic Ocean sector, although in this region the Foreign Office was luckily not involved. In order to mount any expedition to the North Pole, never mind to cross the entire ocean, it was necessary to set out from remote Ellesmere Island in Canada. I could not hope to fly all the necessary equipment to the northern edge of Ellesmere without help from the RAF (who flew empty transport planes on exercises to nearby Greenland), or the USAF, who did likewise from New York. Neither unit would stir themselves without the Canadian Army's go-ahead. They turned us down (as they did every other applicant), since they

The first training site for our polar machines, Scotland, 1975.

maintained a top secret Cold War base at the northern tip of the island.

Another bureaucratic impasse. After four years of soul-destroying attacks on the various authorities, north and south, I had to admit temporary defeat. I wrote then to all 760 sponsors to explain the postponement of the expedition until 1978. This gave me two years' grace to renew the attack, but, by now, Ginnie and I were in penury, as were the other volunteers in the barracks office.

Opposite: Crevasse-crossing trials in Greenland.

Volunteers! These wonderful people included anybody finding themselves at a loose end, who liked the idea of what we were up to and gave their time at no cost helping out in the barracks, listing, storing and packing the growing mountain of stores and rations, but not actually intending to join the expedition team.

During the first two years, we had merely tried to put the project on a war footing; to turn it from a dream into feasible reality no matter what the apparent obstacles. After all, any human being, however meek they might think themselves, can nurture a single-minded desire to fulfil a particular goal. The quantum leap is the moment of instigation, that first push to make the stone roll. Thereafter all manner of unforeseen outside factors will fall into place. In the words of the Scots philosopher William Murray, 'The moment one definitely commits oneself, then Providence moves too. All sorts of things then happen that would otherwise never have occurred.'

Since the idea was for a small group to travel from Greenwich, through both Poles and back to Greenwich without flying one metre of the entire three-year route, I knew we would need two or three very special individuals. How to choose them?

The fewer people the better is my general rule, since human beings are quite badly designed for getting on with each other when under stress. Three or four seemed as small a group as could be expected to do the job.

I asked a polar expert, Colonel Andrew Croft, what team number he advised. 'With three men,' he told me, 'two can gang up on the leader. I would suggest that you, as leader, should only decide whether to have two or three colleagues after you have seen them all in action during Arctic training.'

Since nobody would let us in to the Arctic at the time, I decided North Wales would have to do. Each winter weekend for the next three years, the Territorials provided army trucks and rations for me to train a mountain racing team in Snowdonia and from the team hopefuls, about sixty SAS men in all, I picked the three best ones who applied for the expedition.

Many expeditions, I knew, had foundered through internal schisms brought about through their top-heavy make-up – lots of chiefs and too few Indians. Selection through skills alone could easily end up with big trouble in the ranks. A team of this ilk might typically include a doctor, a mechanic, a navigator, a radio operator, a scientist or two, and, most troublesome of all, a cameraman and film crew. In short, a nest of prima donnas and ingredients likely to curdle.

Better, surely, to search for conventional people with everyday jobs who stand up well to three criteria: level-headedness, patience and good nature towards others.

Some of the
Transglobe
expedition team.
L to R:
Ollie Shepard,
Geoff Newman, RF,
Charlie Burton,
Ginnie and Mike
Wingate Gray.

Ollie in Greenland.

By early 1976, we had narrowed the search to three men: Charlie Burton, a retired corporal from the Sussex Regiment and by then a security officer; Oliver Shepard, a beer salesman; and Geoff Newman, a print expert. None had expedition experience, but all seemed suitable personality-wise, being patient and lacking that all-too-common human complaint of malice which, though usually latent in polite society, surfaces easily in small, confined communities. It leads to bitchiness, petty jealousies, irritability and one-upmanship.

I wanted men who could look after themselves in extreme conditions, possessed plenty of creative energy and initiative, and would normally be selected as leaders in whatever field of activity they chose. Yet an anachronism clearly presented itself here, because any leader will find life a lot easier with natural 'yes-men' rather than a bunch of individualists with a tendency to question any suggested course of action. Balancing different characteristics has always been my aim in team selection and never more so than before Transglobe.

In 1977 Colonel Andrew Croft helped me attract a number of key individuals to form an expedition committee. Sir Vivian Fuchs, who had led the first and only crossing of Antarctica, kindly joined and became pivotal to our ongoing progress. So was Dr John Heap of the Polar Desk at the Foreign Office, and Dr Charles Swithinbank of the British Antarctic Survey. Wally Herbert, who ten years earlier had led the first and only crossing of the Arctic Ocean, became a valued critic and adviser. All these men urged us to gain experience in the Arctic and Greenland (its terrain being similar to Antarctica) before attempting Transglobe.

Right: Arctic Ocean trials, 1976. Camping close to a recent crack is to be avoided if at all possible, a lesson we learned the hard way.

Following their advice and obtaining the necessary extra sponsorship, we spent an additional year in Greenland and the Arctic Ocean learning about the unique obstacles those regions present to the would-be traveller. On our return we spoke with new confidence and our advisers took us more seriously. Now they were prepared to risk their own names to push our case with the authorities. Slowly, very slowly, official doors now began to show chinks of daylight.

Nowadays I am no longer dismayed by official, bureaucratic negatives. I know the best response is to find out how to find a way of appeasing the persons saying 'no' without compromising your own long-term aim and, simultaneously, to befriend other equally weighty officials to fight on your side and help break down the opposition.

The training journeys showed the faults in much of our equipment, which fell to pieces below minus 40°C (the same temperature as minus 40°F). These items we discarded and I located new sponsors with more suitable gear.

In Greenland I watched my own reactions to work at minus 15°C and, of course, those of my three selectees Charlie, Geoff and Oliver. Ginnie and I agreed that Oliver and Geoff were excellent and, therefore, that Charlie would have to go (since I had decided on a travel group of only three, including myself).

Some months later, during our Arctic Ocean trials, the temperature dropped to minus 50°C, at which point Geoff found life difficult. He also suffered frost-bitten fingers, which impaired the circulation in one hand and eliminated him from the team. Charlie was thus firmly established in our land group.

We learned that the snowfields which cover the Antarctic and Greenland landmasses present very different obstacles from the sea-ice which floats on the Arctic Ocean. Tests of our existing snow machines during our trials revealed many misconceptions just in time for me to find sponsors for a different type of snowmobile capable of working at both ends of the world.

Our three-man group would travel by ship over the oceans, by Land Rover in Africa's deserts and jungles, by snowmobile in Antarctica, by twelve-foot rubber boat on Canadian rivers and through the North-West Passage, on foot, ski and snowshoe over Ellesmere Island and by ski, snowmobile and canoe over the Arctic Ocean.

To resupply us over the vast polar ice

Left: Ollie and Charlie in El Golea, Sahara, during a skink hunt.

L to R: Charlie,
RF and Ollie in
the Ivory Coast
forests.

tracts, I signed up two superb ski-plane pilots, one British and one Swiss. The ship's crew consisted of fourteen volunteers from eight countries, each of whom gave up their existing careers to join us for a minimum of three years' unpaid service. One was a USAF colonel, another an Indian First Officer on the P&O line, and a third, from Scotland, was a fully qualified chief engineer.

Knowing nothing about ships, we initially advertised in a shipping magazine for a volunteer crew and the first applicant who we liked the look of was told to find a ship, crew and all relevant equipment, at no cost, in eighteen months. Anton Bowring, previously a deliverer of small craft made in Suffolk, took on this task with two volunteer helpers. By September 1978 things looked sufficiently hopeful, after six years' work, to announce a departure date from Greenwich in twelve months' time.

We now had twenty-five unpaid individuals working full-time, often round the clock, and over 1,900 sponsor companies. As yet we had spent no money at all on the venture, only time and effort.

I kept a tight control, on the basis of Chairman Mao's five-year plans but adding the ingredient of realism, on the activities of each team member. Every three weeks I called them all to the barracks office and ran through the

Opposite:
Eddie Pike doing
maintenance work
on the *Benjy B*
on our way to
Antarctica.
Nobody on the
crew was paid
for three years.

Right: Dave Hicks,
ship's steward,
polishes the
inclinometer. This
instrument was
loaned to the
expedition from
Captain Scott's
ship the *Discovery*
for the duration of
our voyage.

action lists delegated to each person to see who had or had not yet done his or her outstanding tasks. The idle ones were shown up in front of the others and any dangerous signs of unreadiness were focused on immediately. This was designed to avoid a last-minute panic.

Exactly six years after I first began to harass the Foreign Office, I finally received their guarded approval for the Antarctic phase and the Canadian government's seal of approval for the Arctic.

Seven long years after the date of Ginnie's suggestion, we set out from Greenwich with the Patron, HRH The Prince of Wales, at the ship's helm. He wore a black armband because, three days before, his good friend and godfather, Earl Mountbatten, had been killed by the IRA. To the crowd of many thousands of well-wishers Charles said, 'Transglobe is one of the most ambitious undertakings of its kind ever attempted, and the scope of its requirements is monumental. Even though a decade has passed since man set foot on the Moon, polar exploration and research remains as important as ever. As this great journey unfolds, I am confident that this courageous undertaking will provide interest and inspiration to young and old alike throughout the world.' The *New York Times* editorial that day stated, 'The British aren't so weary as they are sometimes said to be. The Transglobe expedition leaves Greenwich, England, today on a journey of such daring that it makes one wonder how the sun ever set on the empire.'

Anton Bowring had recruited and vetted each crew member. Many came from their countries' merchant navies, but the volunteer skipper was a long-retired Royal Navy admiral. Although his name was Otto Steiner, he had helped sink German battleships in the Second World War and was accustomed to ships with disciplined crews.

After driving our Land Rovers south through Europe, we boarded the ship in Barcelona, from whence we were to sail to Algiers. I sensed unease among the crew and Anton confirmed that all was not well. The main cause of dissension was between the admiral and the bosun, previously an ardent trade unionist and shop convenor. A general despondency and lack of unity had then spread among the crew, whose many different nationalities, backgrounds and opinions made them initially resistant to harmony.

With the admiral and Anton present, I held a meeting on deck en route to Africa. I ran through the entire three-year plan and outlined the many problems we were likely to face in living together over the years ahead. I stressed that we, the land group, were no more important to the end goal of the venture than they were. The whole team must strive to work as one or we would certainly fail in the herculean tasks that lay ahead. I ventured some guidelines of patience, tolerance and selflessness which might help, and suggested that anybody who felt they could not take the set-up on board should feel free to leave at Algiers the next day.

Left: The *Benjy B* noses her way south through loose Antarctic pack ice.

The *Benjy B* off
Antarctica.

Ninety-five per cent of the crew stayed on for the full three years of the voyage during which each received a total of three shillings 'Queen's pay'.

The Land Rovers took us through the Sahara, down the lands of the Niger and into the jungles of the Ivory Coast on the western bulge of Africa. At Abidjan, on the Greenwich meridian, we again boarded the ship. Her sponsors were C. T. Bowring of London together with their US partners Marsh & McLennan. Her name was *Benjamin Bowring* or, to all of the crew, simply the *Benjy B*.

Our passage from Cape Town to the Antarctic pack-ice was stormbound and the *Benjy B* behaved sluggishly, laden as she was with over 1,500 45-gallon drums of fuel and her holds bursting with cargo. Only one man on board, a deckhand, had ever been in Antarctic waters before.

Unloading in Antarctica was rushed for fear of a storm as we lay against the ice. Everyone had a specific task, sleeping minimally in shifts, for hundreds of tons of equipment all carefully itemised, numbered and flagged had to be sledged two miles inland and up a natural ice-ramp.

Ginnie had designed pre-fab huts made of cardboard and one was erected at our coastal equipment dump. Two of our support team were to live here for over a year. Soon their hut and all the adjacent lines of equipment (save for the numbered flags on long poles) were covered by snowdrifts. Due to our kit layout plans, made long ago in London, it was nonetheless easy to locate what was needed, whether it be a toothbrush, light bulb or a dozen frozen eggs, by referring to flag and box numbers on the master kit list and then digging what you wanted out of the drifts.

Once the coastal base was ready, the land group went south through the mountains. We travelled with three snowmobiles towing 1,000lb sledges and crossed the crevasse-riven Hinge Zone using techniques we had learned in Greenland. We stopped some 300 miles inland at 6,000 feet above sea level, at the

Left: Ollie and RF running back to the ship at the start of a storm during unloading.

Overleaf: David Mason and Anthony Birkbeck storing drums at Sanae, two miles inland from our landing point.

Ginnie and
Simon Grimes
erecting the
cardboard radio
hut at Ryvingen.

edge of the known world. Over the next three weeks we established a card-board camp and Giles Kershaw, our ski-plane pilot, made over eighty flights from the coastal dump with enough supplies for the four of us to overwinter for eight months. Throughout this static period, including five months of darkness day and night, we would be cut off from all outside assistance. We hoped to keep healthy and to avoid accidents.

The crossing of Antarctica from one side to the other, and unassisted by outside groups, had never yet been achieved. The frozen continent, at 5,500,000 square miles, dwarfs the USA. Seen from outer space, it 'radiates like a great white lantern across the bottom of the world' according to astro-nauts. Only Vivian Fuchs and his snowcat team had crossed Antarctica from edge to edge, and he was assisted by Ed Hillary's tractor team first pioneer-ing an outward route from the Pole. We would be on our own and, using vehicles without cabs, we would be exposed to the extreme cold all the way.

Unknown to us at the time, a sweepstake was set up in the offices of the New Zealand Antarctic Survey. The polar experts there considered our plan under-equipped and our snowmobiles under-powered. They had a map of the continent pinned up with comments appended at appropriate points, such as, 'First crevasse accident', and 'Pulled out here by US Rescue Hercules'. Their general view was 'too far, too high and too cold'.

During that winter of 1980 the winds about our cardboard huts shrieked by at up to 132mph and the wind-chill dropped to minus 130°C. Ginnie's pet Jack Russell terrier helped to keep the four of us sane. There were moments of aggravation, some tiffs and arguments, but very few. Charlie wrote, 'We had worked together closely for a long time. We knew each other's moods and when to lay off. Therefore, the strains were negligible.'

Left: Waving goodbye to the ship. We would not see her again until we had crossed the frozen continent.

Opposite: Ollie Shepard in our 300 yards of stores tunnels during the Antarctic winter.

'When to lay off' is to me an especially important point. Goading people to get back at them or to score points is an everyday human activity which goes on in marriage, in the office and in sport. But it can quickly lead to trouble in the wrong setting and where there is no escape from a confined community. My advice is: 'Don't

Ollie and Bothie
the Jack Russell
inspect our
mock-up crevasse
outside the huts.

take the mickey.' This includes even the light bantering sarcasm which is the standard fare of most non-confined expeditions.

For months on end we lived our lives cramped, damp, dirty, cold and frustrated. The days passed so slowly. The sound of the wind never ceased. An intended joke at the expense of someone feeling low could cause an extreme reaction. At such times the offender had to recognise the danger signs in time to back off and avoid an escalation of dissension.

Equally, this was neither the time nor place to maintain any rigid view-point or stance, if we four, strong individualists were to bear each other's company.

Four was, of course, a better overwintering number than three. Ginnie and I lived together at one end of the hut with an easy relationship and the confidence born of knowing we would never be disloyal to one another. Charlie and Ollie were good enough friends to trust each other likewise. We were two groupings that understood and respected each other's strengths and peculiarities. We knew never to talk about each other disparagingly or to 'whisper behind backs', as that way could too easily spark off a chain of mistrust, suspicion and aggressive isolation in such close confines, where any slight shift in the atmosphere was felt without a word being spoken.

Discipline was hardly necessary, which was just as well since there was no way I could have enforced it, and no threats are infinitely better than idle ones. Our survival in so isolated a spot depended on each person applying self-discipline. We lived in cardboard huts, under the snow, fuelled by petrol. Fire was an ever-present danger, as was carbon monoxide poisoning from our generators. Slops and lavatory bags for four adults over eight months needed careful and ongoing attention. Hundreds of tons of ever-drifting snow required constant shovelling from escape hatches.

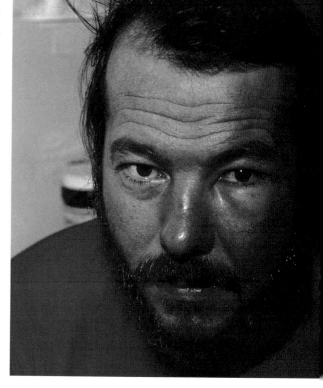

Right: Charlie Burton with frostbite during the Antarctic overwintering.

Leadership, in such circumstances, must be a careful chairmanship conduct-ing an ongoing system of checks. I do not believe in relying on a God-given leader-ship status that will not be challenged. I do believe in constantly looking over my shoulder to ensure any potential challenge to my position is politely, but firmly, seen off. I hold no brief for a split command and, as a great believer in the principle of the thin edge of the wedge, I steer clear of asking for advice since this will usually set a precedent and encourage people to proffer further suggestions when they are not wanted.

I am a severe critic of Roland Huntford's blatantly hostile biography of Scott, but I wholeheartedly agree with his comment, 'In polar expeditions, as in most tight-knit groups, there is usually a process of selecting a natural or psychological leader. It is a conflict akin to a fight for domination within a wolf pack; a more or less overt challenge to the established, formal leadership. How he deals with this threat to his authority is one of the tests through which most commanders have to go . . .'

On 29 October we said goodbye to Ginnie and her dog Bothie and set out to cross Antarctica. The temperature was minus 50°C and the wind a steady 20 knots. Ahead lay over 900 miles of ice where no human had ever trodden since the world was created. This we would map and here, if nowhere else, we would be true explorers.◆

Preparing sleds for the crossing of Antarctica.

The Lessons Learned

Life is too short to waste time on second-class ambitions.
Go for the big ones, even if that means a higher failure rate

◆

At some point in any career, a normally unjustifiable risk
might need to be taken to make the quantum leap from the
mediocre to the big time

◆

When planning for the future and involving unpredictable factors,
such as the weather, allow for the worst-case scenario

◆

Don't be put off by all the apparent obstacles. The very act of starting
the ball rolling will shift quite a few of them

◆

The fewer people involved with any given project the better.
There are very few exceptions to this rule

◆

Whenever feasible, pick your team on character, not skill.
You can teach skills. You can't alter characters

◆

Avoid malicious types at all cost if you're building a team

◆

Balance strengths with care. In avoiding wimpish yes-men you may
take on too many chiefs who don't like being told what to do

◆

Try chewing a few prawns before you announce to the world that you
intend to devour an entire lobster

◆

Avoid last-minute rushes like the plague. Phased planning and
constant checks on progress are the only antidote

◆

Ensure that died-in-the-wool individualists realise that working as part
of the team will in the long term benefit them personally

◆

Survival demands a high level of self-discipline to avoid
the irritation of imposed discipline

◆

Don't ask for advice or suggestions if you don't mean
to follow them up

◆

'There is always a risk in being alive,
and if you are more alive, there is more risk'

IBSEN

4

DICTATOR OR DEMOCRAT

―――――――

My diary, ten days into our crossing, recorded: 'Nobody knows what lies ahead because nobody has been here before.' Back in Britain I had asked the Antarctic experts in Cambridge what was known of the region. 'Previous forays into your area,' they had written, 'have been turned back by crevassing so it seems possible that a lot of the way ahead of you, between 79° and 83° South, may be badly crevassed.' This dearth of surface data had made any careful route planning impossible.

For 600 miles in this unexplored zone we recorded the height of the ice surface above sea level using aneroid barometers, thereby mapping this part of Earth for the first time, and Oliver drilled ten-metre ice cores which, analysed later in Cambridge, would tell the scientists how much snow had fallen here over the past twenty-five years.

Vast regions of sastrugi blocked our path, ridges of ice cut out by the prevailing wind and running transverse to the line of our advance. We struggled over this immense ploughed field, against the grain of ice furrows up to four feet high.

The eighteen-inch skis at the front of our machines jammed in the furrow troughs, as did the heavily laden sledges. We used axes, shovels,

RF in Scott's hut, Antarctica. The bicycle wheels, for measuring distance travelled, were of similar design to those in use in the 1980s.

manpower and foul language to force each mile of painfully slow progress to the south.

The cold was all-pervasive and numbed the brain as well as the extremities. The machines broke down frequently. Springs and bogey wheels shattered and buckled. A supercooled ignition key turned too hard snapped clean off. Oliver, the beer salesman, somehow managed to cope with each successive mechanical trouble. The hard lessons he had learned during our previous polar trials proved invaluable. As we climbed to 11,000 feet above sea level the engines were increasingly affected by the thin air. We slowed to the pace of anaemic snails and ran out of fuel within ten miles of our expected minimum range.

While our ski-plane flew fuel drums from the coastal dump, we camped and waited for seventeen days. The mathematics were critical. To stock up a fuel cache in the middle of nowhere and often flying blind in blizzard conditions, our pilot Giles made ten flights amounting to 12,000 miles in ninety-two hours, using up 6,000 gallons. Only twenty-five drums now remained of the 1,100 we had shipped from Cape Town the previous year, and Giles had to use up twelve to fly just one to the Pole, the halfway point of our crossing journey.

In Antarctica the key to any project is the cost of the aviation fuel for support aircraft. At the time of writing, one 45-gallon drum costs US$120 in Chile, US$6,000 by the time it reaches Antarctica and US$25,000 when it ends up at the Pole.

Navigation was a problem every minute of the day in this featureless land. For 1,200 miles I used the sun, my watch and a compass with nothing solid to aim at or check against. This problem was compounded by many days of white-out including the day we finally reached the American research station at the South Pole.

My means of determining our daily position was a theodolite and complex navigation tables. This kit weighed 32lb. (In the 1980s I switched to a 2lb plastic sextant, thanks to research work into plastics at low temperatures and, after 1991, I began to use a GPS or satellite positioning device which weighed less than nine ounces.)

We stayed for four days at the South Pole station waiting for Ginnie and her radio gear to be flown there by Giles. A merry Christmas, planned by the twelve resident scientists, was only a day away, but we needed every hour if we were to complete the crossing during Antarctica's brief summer season. Each day of delay increased the hazards ahead. Summer was already well advanced. Crevasse bridges, sun-weakened, would be increasingly liable to

Charlie shovels
snow into the
water tank as the
sun returns to
Ryvingen after
a five-month
absence.

cave in beneath us. Robert Scott, sixty-nine years before, had left this place at the bottom of the world two or three days too late and, stranded by early blizzards, had died as a result.

On 2 March, the last ships and aircraft would have to leave Antarctica or risk being marooned there for eight months. After that date our own situation would revert to that of Scott's group, with zero possibility of rescue or supply.

I noticed an unusual tension in the tent as we approached the edge of the high plateau. Ahead of us lay a 180-mile cliff-girt chute, the Scott glacier, which dropped through 9,000 feet of chaotic ice to the coastal edge of Antarctica.

One of the most treacherous zones of this glacier, never previously descended, was its upper rim. A white-out caught us in an area of great instability so we camped fully aware that a hidden network of trapdoors to oblivion lay all about us. Slits and caverns with inch-thin booby traps, snow covers hiding dizzy drops of 150 feet and more.

Knowing that a weather change could pin us down for two precious weeks, I decided that delay posed a greater danger than attempting to travel blind.

Charlie and Ollie dig out a sledge after an overnight blizzard.

Ollie was silent when I announced this, but Charlie, to use Ollie's words, 'was very shirty as he thought we should have stayed in the tent and not travelled in the white-out through the crevasse field'. Whenever my decisions appeared to the others to be wrong, Charlie was an excellent weather-vane. On this occasion I could see his point. To move through a highly volatile zone, unable to spot the hazards ahead or underfoot, could be described as stupid but, in my opinion, we ran a much greater long-term danger if we lost the race against the onrush of polar winter due to short-term caution.

If I was misunderstood through not fully communicating the logic of my decision, the fault was doubly mine, since my reason for failing to 'discuss options' was merely the desire to avoid an argument that might not win me the most votes.

In a way my past life had cushioned me from having to explain myself to others, especially the years in the Arab army. The Omanis had accepted my instant decisions and changes of mind without question. Reacting to quick-change military situations such as lethal ambushes did not involve a democratic decision-making process with the men.

But Oliver and Charlie were not accustomed to blindly following orders they could not understand. Neither were they, like the majority of the navy men with Scott and Shackleton, trained to obey without question. On the contrary, they were strong individualists and leaders of men, who disliked being told what to do at the best of times. They expected involvement in planning our moves.

Normally I respected this and many a democratic decision took place over the years between the three of us but, when instant action and reaction was required, I reverted to the one-man-band-ism to which the army had accustomed me. For one thing, it saved precious time.

There was also another, more subtle factor, which sometimes stirred the chemicals between the three of us. Urgency. Charlie and Ollie were brought up by their parents in the old-fashioned way. Faced with danger they consciously avoided at all costs any outward show of haste as though it was a symbol of cowardice; as though to hurry in the face of adversity would be unseemly and ungentlemanly.

I believe my father would have had just such an effect on my own behaviour had he survived the war and guided my formative years. As it was, I had developed my own, perhaps maverick, policies and these did not include having a democratic pow-wow with my companions, however brief, when some imminent hazard demanded a speedy reaction. If I was confident that my way was best, what would be the point of a discussion to listen to other possible ways?

Giles Kershaw in the Twin Otter buzzes the crossing team as it nears Mount Erebus.

The surest way I know of 'leading leaders', without suffering successive confrontations, is to be entirely sure of yourself and to know that nobody had more experience than you do at the job in hand.

So we broke camp, crept forward and, luckily, the white-out lifted. Charlie, careful never to sound excited about anything, described the

RF coaxing his
skidoo up an
incline in soft
snow.

subsequent journey: 'The descent was hair-raising, too steep for the sledges which ran down ahead of our skidoos, sometimes wrenching them sideways, even backwards, over wide, droopy snowbridges. Some of these bridges had fracture lines on both sides and were obviously ready to implode at the first excuse. How we made the bottom God only knows.'

We continued day after day with few solid areas of respite. One disturbed region averaged a crevasse every six yards, two-thirds of which had lost their bridges. Oliver wrote, 'The descent was a nightmare. Ran zigzagged in all directions to avoid the worst but with little success. At one point today we ended in a major pressure zone with great ice bubbles and blue domes rearing above us as we slithered along a maze of cracked corridors, totally lost. I could mention a hundred such incidents but what's the point . . . Nobody who wasn't there, who hasn't felt a snowbridge begin to fall away directly beneath his skidoo seat, who hasn't been forced to carry on hour after hour, day after day, through the world's worst crevasse fields can even imagine the extreme fear of it all.'

Against the expectations of polar pundits in many countries, we made the descent without loss of life and, in nine days, crossed the Ross Ice Shelf to Scott Base on the continent's Pacific rim. We had traversed the Antarctic continent in sixty-seven days; the first one-way-only crossing of Antarctica ever made.

Giles, our resupply pilot, had saved the lives of a number of lost South African scientists during our journey. He was awarded the Guild of Pilots Sword of Honour. Sadly, flying a gyrocopter, he died in Antarctica some years later. He was known for his polar expertise and his critical nature, vital to a good polar pilot. Of Transglobe he said, 'Before we even left London, I really doubted they would succeed. Their land team are after all not professionals at anything. I mean, they have learned to cook in Charlie's case, how to be a mechanic in Ollie's, and Ginnie, how to be a radio operator. Ran is a good leader, probably a great leader, but he has had to learn about navigation. The great thing about these four people is their persistence as a group in the face of terrible difficulties in getting across; not their individual abilities.'

Unfortunately, any collective ability we may have developed as a group was soon to be reduced. Oliver's American wife had become very worried about his continued absence in risky places and, after much deliberation, he had regretfully responded to her urgings by agreeing to leave Transglobe.

The committee in London decided to find an army replacement for Oliver. Sir Vivian Fuchs and Mike Wingate Gray, the ex-SAS CO, flew to meet us in New Zealand. They were completely against Charlie and I

Overleaf:

The crossing team

approaches Mount

Erebus on Ross

Island.

attempting the Arctic as a two-man group. I was equally adamant that Oliver should only be replaced if I found that the two of us alone could not cope. Charlie was not over-fussy, but was inclined to favour two not three.

Arguing my point, I quoted Wally Herbert, leader of the only expedition ever to cross the Arctic Ocean, who wrote, 'As a two-man party we would travel harder, faster and more efficiently than as a three-man unit.'

The committee members looked unimpressed. 'More importantly,' I added, 'Charlie and I have worked together now for six years. We know each other's limitations and plus points. We have a mutually acceptable *modus vivendi*. However well we may know some third person in normal circumstances, he may turn out very different given the unique stress of Arctic Ocean travel. Quite apart from any personality interaction between us and such a "third man", his very presence could easily undermine our own mutual compatibility.'

The committee, however, remained doggedly against our attempting the ambitious journey ahead without a third man. In desperation, I did what I always do in such straits: appealed directly to the boss. In the case of Transglobe the relevant god was our Patron, HRH The Prince of Wales. Due to the time difference I had to call him at his Gloucestershire home well after

Charlie's sledge jammed on three-foot-high sastrugi.

midnight and he sounded groggy. I put the 'third man' problem to him and his response was unequivocal. He was due to visit us in Sydney in a fortnight and he promised he would put my point of view strongly to the committee.

It would have been easy for the Prince to suggest we solve our own problems but, because he did act as final arbiter for the expedition, we were able to sort out such matters in a friendly manner by passing the buck upwards to someone whose judgement we all respected.

By now there were fourteen learned people on the London committee. Captain Scott once said of his own expedition committee: 'Too many cooks spoil the broth and too many men on the committee are the devil.' On the other hand, without the backing of these eminent individuals, the expedition would never have set foot in Antarctica. Their time, advice and support was

Ginnie in her radio hut. Sometimes she kept non-stop radio watch for thirty-six hours. Over the two-month crossing journey, she averaged three hours' sleep daily.

freely given and, were they to agree to everything the field leader proposed, there would be little point in their existence.

Charlie saw things slightly differently. He wrote: 'Ran runs the show. He is the leader in the field . . . If he wants to do something, he does it and the committee, they try to change it. I think this is the first time he has had people who feel they should organise him. This is unfortunate for him and he feels the strain. I can see this.'

With the Prince's involvement the issue was finally resolved and we continued as a two-man group. Sir Vivian Fuchs made it clear that if things went wrong as a result, the burden of irresponsibility would be entirely mine.

The *Benjy B* chugged her way north past Fiji. A vessel designed for polar conditions, her crew and especially the engineers boiled in the leaden heat of the tropics. At one point we stopped in mid-Pacific and everybody jumped overboard, including Ginnie's dog, but even the sea felt warm and sticky.

We came at length to the Bering Straits and the ship ventured into the silted shallows off the mouth of the Yukon river. To the north her way was blocked by Arctic sea-ice so the plan, made eight years before, was to drop the travel group overboard in rubber boats. We would then go up the Yukon,

Reunited with the ship: the volunteers of the Transglobe team.

down the MacKenzie, through the North-West Passage and north through the islands of the Canadian archipelago to the most northerly habitation in Canada, our old training base at Alert on Ellesmere Island.

Because, in a 'bad' year, the Yukon river only unfreezes in the third week of June, all our plans to boat up that river were scheduled accordingly. However, the sea-ice in the Canadian archipelago often freezes in early September. Unless we managed to keep to a rigid rate of progress for over

**Charlie, off the
mouth of the
Yukon, minutes
before his capsize.**

**Overleaf:
Our Progress
through the North-
West Passage.**

2,000 hazardous river and sea miles, we would end up frozen into the sea somewhere west of Greenland.

Our two twelve-foot rubber boats were winched overboard in choppy waters sixteen miles off the Yukon. The ship had already 'hit bottom' so she could go no closer to the Alaskan coast. A rogue wave overturned Charlie's heavily laden inflatable and near disaster ensued. Back on the ship we watched as the skipper edged around wicked shoals until, 200 miles further north, we anchored off the Indian sea village of St Michael. This time our boats made it to the coast and at length to a tributary of the Yukon but Charlie's earlier dunking, within view of the *Benjy B*, had forced me to rethink my plans for boating the infamous North-West Passage in the rubber inflatables. The problem was that the loads we each had to carry were just too heavy due to Oliver's absence. I had planned to divide our gear between three, not two, boats. The only solution was to switch to a different type of boat which would cope with our load and the Arctic storms of the Passage. From an Indian village I radioed Ginnie, then working as a maid and wait-ress at the Klondike Lodge near Dawson City. This was timely employment as she had no funds, a sponsored Land Rover towing five 45-gallon fuel drums on a trailer, her Jack Russell terrier and, in two weeks' time, the job of

transporting us and our boats from a bridge 600 miles up the Yukon to Inuvik on the MacKenzie river.

'We will need a nineteen-foot Boston whaler boat with outboards once we get to Inuvik,' I told her. 'The inflatables will simply not cope with our heavy loads in the big seas of the Passage.'

In between making beds and serving meals, Ginnie telephoned desperately around the world to find a boat sponsor. After five days she located a banker in Hong Kong who agreed to buy us a whaler. Frantic work then ensued back in Vancouver, the nearest source of a Boston whaler, and the current berth of the *Benjy B*. Two of the ship's crew supervised ice-modifications to the new whaler and Ginnie found a cargo plane boss willing to underwrite its trans-port to Inuvik. Its arrival there coincided with ours so no time was lost.

Left: RF and Charlie pass an Indian fish-trap on the Yukon river.

Opposite: RF and Charlie thread their way through the floating ice of the North-West Passage.

When I had told our boating expert, Anton Bowring, of my plan to switch from the inflatables to an open whaler, he had advised against it. 'I personally think that a whaler is not a clever move,' he wrote. 'Its use to Ran is going to be very limited as it will only be useful in open ice-free water. It weighs 1,500lb plus the weight of forty gallons of fuel and two 60hp engines of 260lb each. It will be quite impossible to manhandle across ice-floes and it cannot be flown anywhere in a float-plane so they will have to ditch it before they have got halfway. The engines will use up eight gallons of fuel per hour. Even if they can do 25 knots they will be reduced to a crawl in rough seas or risk breaking its back.'

But I was convinced a whaler was our only chance now that my inflatables plan had proved ill-conceived. There have been many occasions, on many expeditions, when the experts have counselled against the plan I thought best for the problem ahead. When this happens I try to keep an open mind, always plan for the worst-case scenario, balance all the likely factors against each other and then go for the best compromise solution. Once the decision is then made, I push it hard and fast and try to forget the ominous warnings of doom from the experts whose advice I have had to ignore.

Advice and dire warnings from the local experts came thick and fast

when Charlie and I finally reached the Arctic mouth of the MacKenzie river at Tuktoyaktuk. We said good-bye to Ginnie there on 26 July. In the thirty-five summer days left when, with luck, the Passage should remain at least partially ice-free, we must complete not only the 3,000 miles of the Passage, in which so many ships and men have disappeared, but also cover an additional 500 miles still further to the north. We must reach somewhere within skiing distance of our Arctic winter quarters, before the new ice began to crust over the sea forcing us to abandon the whaler. Great icebreakers crash through the ice between the islands of the archipelago, but small boats have only navigated the Passage a dozen times averaging three consecutive summer seasons to do so.

Navigation was a problem. The latest chart was overprinted in large

Left: The whaler is frozen into the sea-ice of Tanquary fjord. From here RF and Charlie had to continue by ski.

Opposite: Charlie making his way through a frozen valley on Ellesmere Island.

letters 'MAGNETIC COMPASS USELESS IN THIS AREA'. I visited a Tuktoyaktuk barge captain for advice. 'Don't go,' he said. 'That's the best course for you. My barge has radar beacon responders, MF and DF, and we stay out in the deep channels. But you must hug the coastline to escape the storms so you will hit the shoals. Also, you must stick along the jagged coastline, which looks like the graph of an erratic heartbeat. So you'll have to go much further and need fuel where there is none. Most of the time it will be thick fog so you'll want to use a compass. But you can't.'

The first month of travel was a hectic and uncomfortable race with little sleep. I spent much of the time frightened. If the rolling waves capsized us, as I often thought they would, we would undoubtedly die in the water. Long stretches of coastline offered no landing spot and the tundra everywhere was uninhabited but for isolated radar sites.

One especially nerve-racking day took us past some forty miles of burning cliffs. Sulphur deposits, forever on fire, glowed red and yellow plumes of smoke rose from deep crevices above the roar and grind of the angry surf.

On 30 July we ploughed east for thirty-six hours, without a break, for the cliffs that we skirted faced north with no stitch of cover. We were very tired, wet, cold and always cramped together. Charlie was later asked how we got

on. 'We do lose our tempers occasionally,' he replied, 'but very, very seldom and mainly when under pressure.'

At the next settlement we learned that ice blocked our way east so we detoured south a hundred miles in 30-knot winds and fog. We sheltered from one gale on a tiny island, but on 3 August my patience gave out and we ran through the storm. In a mist we grounded on shoals in the lee of dark cliffs. We escaped by luck, but that evening there were no more islands to dodge between, and we plunged all night between creaming breakers. Twice the whole, heavy boat was flung into the darkness as great walls of water struck us broadside.

More by luck than good management we limped exhausted into the isolated radar station at Gladman Point. The station boss said we must now wait for the storm to abate

Charlie on Ellesmere Island after cutting his forehead on a rock.

as, to the east, the big seas in Wellington and Victoria Straits would be lethal. We learned on his radio that the local Eskimo fishermen had been stranded for five days. 'You must wait,' he advised us. 'The Eskimos know best.'

I had no wish to ignore local knowledge, but winter was closing in fast. On 13 August we reached the Passage's halfway point at the Eskimo village of Gjoa Haven.

I knew I would one day write a book about the journey and had Charlie's agreement I could quote from his diary. While he was away from our shelter I thumbed through his more recent jottings and, when he returned, confronted him. 'Why,' I prodded his diary, 'do you say that I was lost last week?'

'Because you told me that you were.'

'Yes, but I meant our exact position between two river mouths, not generally lost in the North-West Passage!'

We argued heatedly about the word 'lost' and its connotations, but our general rule was to avoid confrontation unless there was some controversial principle likely to develop into a festering resentment if not openly discussed.

We came to a forty-mile crossing packed with highly mobile ice-floes. Fog descended and a north wind blew the ice towards us. There was no shelter since the coast was lined by sheer cliffs. Rather than risk being crushed in the ice-pack, I told Charlie that we must turn back and search for the protection of a narrow fjord. He looked most disgruntled and silence reigned. I was tempted to argue the issue, but I knew this would be a pointless exercise since I was sure mine was the correct course.

Charlie had often been unhappy when I had progressed despite known risks. The opposite was now

Heading north up the newly frozen Lake Hazen on Ellesmere Island.

true. The whole affair of judging risks can be a touch intuitive and, when time is critical, I will respond to my natural inclination even though others present are strongly advising an alternative course. One key principle I hold dear, a policy much beloved by the late Field Marshal Montgomery, is never to move against opposition until the cards appear stacked in your favour. Nature can be a tough 'opponent' not given to handing out second chances

RF and Charlie get
ready to leave the
Alert huts for the
attempt to cross
the Arctic Ocean.

if you get it wrong the first time, so I seldom take risks if a reasonable alternative course is still open.

We were pinioned in a fjord for four anxious days, but a wind change then loosened the ice and we pushed north through a labyrinth of floes to Resolute Bay. Again the ice blocked our way north, which was worrying since only six days remained before the sea was likely to freeze over. Pack ice already seemed to surround us. In a few days we would face a nine-month delay until the following summer so, taking the bull by horns, we set out on an unprecedented 900-mile journey with small chance of success.

Much of the next five days saw us bouncing through rough seas, dwarfed by huge jostling icebergs and sheer black cliffs. For one period of nine hours we saw no landing place, no inlet, however small. Our propeller blades broke, one by one, against unseen chunks of growler ice and our speed lessened hour by hour.

Charlie spotted a tiny defile, the size of a suburban garden, between two cliffs. In desperation we nosed towards it to change propellers only to find a polar bear already in residence hunting for beluga whales. Since an unbroken cliff-line stretched east and north for at least the next twenty miles, we nosed in beside the bear and warily changed propellers.

For 120 miles we bucked and rolled between huge icebergs. Some, bigger than bungalows, rolled about like beach balls in the 60-knot gale and freezing sleet.

Back at Resolute Ginnie maintained an unsleeping vigil on her radio, well aware of our vulnerability along these wild, remote coastlines. When I managed to contact her, two days behind schedule, I could hear the tiredness and stress in her voice.

RF fights to save his skidoo from a long drop to the bottom of the Arctic Ocean.

I found our intended route through Hell's Gate Passage ice-blocked, so we detoured around Devil Island to the only alternative sea-canyon. By the skin of our teeth we squeezed by giant grounded bergs into Norwegian Bay. Two anxious days and nights later we reached Great Bear Cape as the sea's surface, all around us, began to congeal. Desperately in need of warmth and sleep, we had no choice but to keep going for the last 230 northerly miles of interlocking fjords.

A strong wind kept the new ice from forming in the sea-fjords through the night of 30 August and, by the dawn of the new month, we saw to our north the dead-end beach of Tanquary fjord. Snow-capped peaks now blocked our way north. Wolves stared from lava beaches, but nothing moved except us, shattering with our wash the mirror-images of the dark valley walls.

Within four days the boat was frozen into the bay. It was to remain there undisturbed for seven years. With 100lb loads we skied north over the mountains of Ellesmere Island, switching to snowshoes on steep, icy sections. For 150 miles we passed no man-made object, no paths, nothing but rock and ice. In one valley our only route lay under a glacier passing through a blue tunnel carved out by melt water.

Charlie cut his head open on a rock and deep blisters festered on the soles of both his feet. Our boots broke through the snow's crust into hidden holes and Charlie jarred his spine. His left eye was swollen shut and his right heel was raw with weeping poison. He no longer wanted to carry his rifle.

'What about bears?' I asked him.

'Good thing,' he muttered, 'they'd put me out of my misery.'

We crossed over an unnamed mountain range at 2,000 feet and, late on 15 September, reached the foot of Omingmak Mountain, disturbing a herd of musk oxen which galloped off, snorting.

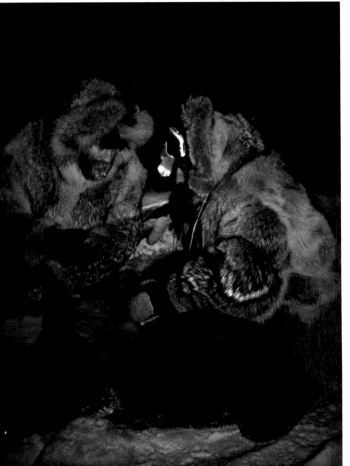

With Charlie's feet and back torturing him, we climbed west of the weird tundra polygons of Black River Vale, close by Fort Conger on the coast. In 1924 the American explorer Greely wintered in a hut there. He and his men suffered slow starvation, insanity, cannibalism and death.

Every day grew colder and the daylight hours rapidly diminished. Freezing fog banks closed over the glaciers and we camped beneath the Boulder Hills at 2,200 feet in a narrow, frozen gully. The temperature dropped to minus 20°C as, by good luck, we located the hidden entrance to the narrow rock-girt corridor dropping into the upper canyon of the Grant river which

RF and Charlie confer. Hearing anything above the screech of the wind was often difficult.

falls for thirty miles to the very edge of the continental landmass.

At noon on 26 September, the riverbed plunged down a frozen waterfall, and a jagged vista of contorted pack-ice stretched away to the polar horizon, the Arctic Ocean.

Travelling east along the edge of the semi-frozen sea, we came by dusk to the twin huts of Alert, the most northerly buildings in the world. We had travelled around the polar axis of the world for 314° of latitude in 750 days. Only 46° more now to Greenwich, but by far the most perilous sector lay ahead.

Within a few days winter arrived at Alert, the temperature plummeted and the sun disappeared. For the next five months Ginnie, Charlie and I, with Ginnie's dog, lived in the huts at Alert and planned the final phase, the crossing of the Arctic Ocean via the North Pole.

Within yards of our beds, the sea-ice in the bay creaked and groaned in the dark. At times major upheavals and tidal surges cracked the floes apart and the ominous roar of a million tons of ice on the move kept us awake. Soon we would be spending six months trying to traverse 2,000 miles of 'that stuff', as Charlie called it.

No man had ever crossed the Arctic Ocean in a single season, as we must; the only crossing in history, four men with forty dogs under Wally Herbert, had taken two summer seasons.

By the 1990s the Poles and Mount Everest had become tourist destinations, but back in 1982 only a few individuals had attempted to reach the North Pole, and they had done so with light loads, aided by resupply and ski-plane removal from the Pole before the annual break-up of the floes. Because we

RF and Charlie struggle north over the rubble.

were attempting to go over twice the mere distance to the Pole prior to the break-up, we needed to set out well before any of our predecessors. Instead of waiting for the comparative comfort of March, with sunlight and warmer temperatures, we must set out in mid-February in twenty-four-hour darkness and temperatures in the minus 50s.

We left Ginnie on 13 February, with a wind-chill factor of minus 90°C blowing in our faces. Four days later we found our way west along the coast blocked by pressure ice so we turned north on to the sea-ice. For days we axed and shovelled a way between ice walls and boulders for our skidoos and heavy sledges. By 19 February we had slowed to a crawl and I made a snap decision to abandon the skidoos for later collection by ski-plane. We continued immediately, dragging our key stores on man-haul sledges. Our progress through the twilit gloom at once accelerated.

Sheer exhaustion overcame any fear of bears and a competitive sense helped us work for long hours, for we knew a Norwegian team would soon be setting out to beat us across the Arctic.

One night back at base, Ginnie woke to find our main store hut on fire. She tried to put out the flames, probably ignited by an electrical spark, but, with rifle bullets and flares exploding about her, she had to desist, and by morning everything was destroyed.

Although to this point the entire expedition had attracted little media attention, despite its success, our base-camp fire sparked immediate interest all over the world.

Within an hour of assessing the damage Ginnie began a forty-eight-hour sleepless vigil on her radio to London and, inside ten days, our sponsors there reacted with replacement equipment, everything from rations to parachutes.

All our resupply gear for the Arctic crossing was destroyed in the Alert fire.

In the evening of 7 March, my thirty-eighth birthday, in our tiny tent on the ice, we celebrated with two extra cigarettes. That day Charlie's diary recorded: 'We suck ice and snow. There are times when Ran and I have to camp exhausted because we can't pick the axes up. We are shattered. But there is always light at the tunnel's end and that is what you must think about.'

We averaged seven miles of northerly progress each day with the man-haul sledges. When at length the ski-plane brought back our skidoos, we reverted to a mere mile at best, but I knew that once the rubble-belt thinned out the skidoos would come into their own on the longer, flatter floes.

One day in March, in poor light, I steered my skidoo into a canal. Within minutes the machine was underwater and the sledge soon followed. We continued with Charlie's gear but, without the tent, life was about as

**Charlie crosses
a pressure ridge
north of Cape
Columbia.**

miserable as I had thought possible. A sudden storm broke up the ice-floes and a sea of dirty sludge moved across the broken edge of our floe. Thick fog then descended.

Back in London a committee report stated, 'At this stage it is fair to say that nobody involved in the expedition would give much for its chances of reaching the Pole this year.'

On 21 March our Norwegian rivals ran into trouble and one, who was suffering from frostbite, was eventually rescued. The other two men continued, but they failed in their crossing attempt. By now Charlie and I were both suffering from lack of sleep, piles, many areas of raw skin, bloodshot eyes, swollen and bloody fingers, toes, noses and lips, crotch rot, cracked fillings and a variety of other discomforts. But there was no serious damage, so we began to make good progress as the ice rubble lessened.

Early in April, at 87° 48' North, only 130 miles from the Pole, we were stopped by the most massive wall I had ever seen in the Arctic. But now we had refined our wall-crossing and axing techniques and traversed it in only four hours. To our north the ice-floes began to crack up. On 8 April, my diary recorded, 'Crossed 62 cracks today but the bit is between our teeth. Twenty-one miles done.'

We reached the top of the world half an hour before midnight, on Easter Day, 10 April. We were the first men in history to have travelled over the Earth's surface to both Poles, but many hundreds of miles and cold, wet months still lay between us and the *Benjy B*.

I estimated that the break-up would begin within the next four weeks. In this time we must reach the edge of the Arctic sea-ice, somewhere near Spitsbergen, and the safety of the ship. Or, if that were to prove impossible, we must locate a large thick-ice floe and hope to float south on it. After the break-up only the largest, strongest floes can hope to survive the chaos of overall fracturing caused by pressure within the pack.

Two weeks after leaving the Pole we reached 86° 10' North, completing some 230 miles of southerly progress, but all around us the sea was opening up. I knew we must find a safe floe before the break-up began, but Charlie felt we should concentrate on getting much further south before even looking for safe floes. Otherwise, he believed, we would be cut off from any

Left: At the North Pole, Easter Day, 1982. We became the first people to reach both poles by surface travel.

Opposite: The crew fraternise with a local as the *Benjy B* picks her way through heavy Arctic pack-ice.

Overleaf: The ice group at last reaches the *Benjy B* to complete the first circumnavigation of the Earth's polar axis.

hope of reaching the ship before the ice re-froze in four months' time. We discussed our options and I took the safer course of searching for a floe sooner rather than later.

Charlie made his position clear. The decision was mine not his. The outcome of starting to float too soon from too far north might make us end up well short of the ice-edge and the *Benjy B*. If so, all fingers would point at me.

The popular course would be to bash on. But the southerly sea currents were now with us. I used a 1936 Soviet guide, which showed a good mathematical chance that we could float south fast enough to just make it. My natural instinct to hurry on conflicted with an inner instinct to be cautious. The outcome of ten years of work by many people depended on this single decision.

The ensuing search for a suitable floe was nearly our undoing. Charlie and I both ended up on the same narrow stretch of mobile sludge towing all our gear. We came to within a few yards of breaking through into the sea. Nothing could have saved us and I cannot to this day forget the nightmare of that moment.

At last we located a solid floe and made camp. Although there were many scares over the next three months of floating and many new cracks which slowly diminished the floe's size, it took us safely south despite the frequent storms that raged about our fragile home.

Nineteen bears visited the tent over our ninety-five days on the floe. Only one was aggressive and he was warned off by a bullet through the shin as he attacked.

During the entire duration of our Arctic Ocean journey, Charlie and I had no flare-ups or periods of bad atmosphere. The secret was probably the long period of working together prior to starting the crossing. We were able to recognise each other's stress points so well that we knew almost subconsciously when to steer clear of a delicate topic.

On 1 June, Charlie, checking his diary in the tent, muttered, 'By tonight we will have been travelling from Greenwich for 1,000 days.'

Due to strong, southerly winds, our float rate slowed to a crawl and the committee in London worked out that we could not reach any point where we might rendezvous with the ship before that winter. On 2 July the ship tried to force her way towards us but was driven back. Later than month, eighty-two miles from our floe, the *Benjy B* struck ice too hard and a key welding joint in the stern cracked open. Cleverly, the captain managed to ram another floe in such a way as to run the damaged section high out of the water and, kneeling on the floe, the engineers botched up a temporary repair.

In mid-July the committee, very worried that we would soon be out of reach in the pack-ice, sent orders to Ginnie that the ski-plane must try to evacuate us. But Ginnie developed sudden radio troubles and failed to receive this evacuation order. At the end of the month, when a wind change briefly loosened the pack, the *Benjy B* tried again.

On 3 August she became jammed only seventeen miles from our floe. At 2pm that afternoon we abandoned the floe and, using two small canoes on detachable skis, made a dash for the ship on a compass bearing. The canoe skis broke, but we hauled like madmen and, mounting a pressure ridge at 7pm, I spotted two tiny matchsticks to the south, the masts of the *Benjy B*.

I think that was the single most satisfactory moment of my life. For three hours we heaved, tugged, paddled and often lost sight of the ship, but soon after midnight we climbed on board. The circle was complete.

Ginnie was standing by a cargo hatch. Between us we had spent twenty years to reach this point. None of us will forget that moment – we shared then something that no one could ever take away from us.

On 24 August Prince Charles brought the ship back to her starting point at Greenwich, almost three years to the day since we had set out. Ten thousand cheering people lined the banks. The journey was over. Earth had been circumnavigated on her polar axis.

I learned many lessons from Transglobe, and one was never to rest on my laurels. At the time of our success we were exhausted. The team quickly melted away back to their own countries and homes. They needed to earn a living and to resume their broken careers. The temptation to take a holiday ourselves, for we were very tired,

The Transglobe patron, HRH The Prince of Wales, greets RF and Charlie at Greenwich.

was great but, had we done so, all the years of effort would have gone to waste in terms of our long-term aims.

There is but a short period after an event like Transglobe when the public are curious and keen to know all about it. Their memories are very short and plenty of other attractions constantly compete for their attention. The key is to make the most of the brief time-span when you still have that attention. For us that time was exceptionally short due to an accident of fate. Coinciding with our 'heroic arrival' at Greenwich from the polar north, Mrs Thatcher's PR machine was working furiously to trumpet the simultaneous return of 'our brave boys' at Portsmouth from the polar south or, to be precise, the Falklands War. As a result, we learned the valuable lesson that, in terms of public perception, it is the media who decide the value of what you accomplish, not the actual scope of your deeds.

It is difficult to give a day-to-day example of this without offending someone, but I will try. In Britain we have a string of men who have achieved extremely difficult polar and mountain firsts by skill and tenacity over the past three decades and yet, because they failed to organise sufficient media coverage of their achievements, few people even in England appreciate what they have done. These men, in addition to those named elsewhere in this book, include Robert Swan, Geoff Somers, Joe Simpson and Roger Mear.

After Transglobe I made sure that subsequent expeditions were well featured in the media since, if they weren't, I would not be able to make a living, because my books about the journeys would not sell well and, even

more critically, I would not receive the lecture contracts which were my bread and butter.

The logic was simple business. The agencies took a percentage of every lecture so they favoured the speakers who were requested the most. Nearly every conference organiser wanting a speaker would choose, from the agency lists, people who were in the public eye. This remains true today.

I failed to recognise this basic commercial factor on the Transglobe expedition, which had no public relations agency involvement.

The corollary to this point is that however major any particular achievement may be, it will only be a transient success in the eyes of the public and you cannot, even briefly, rest on the laurels of it. As they say in the film industry, 'You are only as good as your next movie.'◆

Selling off equipment at Camden Lock market in order to pay off the expedition debts.

The Lessons Learned

Watch out for the temptation of lingering too long in a warm hut when
your schedule is tight and the weather may change.
Likewise don't put off uncomfortable business decisions when a
window of opportunity briefly presents itself

◆

Balance short-term caution against long-term dangers.
Maybe it is best to press on today, even if the conditions are risky,
to avoid delay causing even greater hazards tomorrow

◆

If there is time, take extra trouble to explain with care those decisions
and orders most likely to be unpopular

◆

The most certain way of maintaining control over
difficult individuals is to be entirely self-confident because you know
you are better at the job in hand than they are

◆

Adding a new individual to a small group that work well together
must be done with tact and caution

◆

Never waste time applying to the boss's secretary
if you can go straight to the boss

◆

When you can't make up your mind and the experts' advice
is contradictory, keep an open mind, balance all likely factors,
plan for a bad scenario and go for the best compromise solution.
Then, once you've made your decision, stick to your guns

◆

Avoid argument except where a matter is likely to develop into
festering resentment if not confronted

◆

Try never to move against the opposition until the cards
are stacked in your favour

◆

There are times when it is better to err on the side of caution just as,
at other times, the risk option is preferable. In either case the leader
needs to trust his instinct – based, ideally, on experience

◆

Never rest on your laurels if you have rivals

◆

'*Thinking makes it so*'

WILLIAM SHAKESPEARE

5

LATERAL
THOUGHT

For three years Ginnie and I had travelled the world eating sponsored Transglobe rations. In our absence the cost of Flora margarine in London had doubled. And there were other similar cultural shocks to absorb on our return, mostly to do with living costs.

The day we settled back into the expedition office, a member of the volunteer staff showed us the books. Somehow, Transglobe was £120,000 in debt. To us, a vast sum. All the team and the volunteers left to resume their careers apart from Anton Bowring, who said, 'The expedition will not be complete until the debts are paid off. If you like, I'll help out until they are.' For the next eighteen months Anton and Ginnie worked full-time to raise funds. One of their schemes which did well was a street-market sale of left-over expedition food and equipment at Camden Lock market; everything from mustard pots to shovels.

I stayed at home to write a book about Transglobe. We soon ran into lean times, since neither of us had time to earn a living. By the time the book was written and the debts paid off, our financial predicament was acute. We needed to start planning a new expedition, but mortgage and other bills got in the way by demanding that I earn some income without delay.

RF with Dr Armand Hammer.

At 4am one morning, in the autumn of 1984, I was woken by a call from Los Angeles and offered the job of Public Relations Officer at Occidental Petroleum. The caller was Dr Armand Hammer, octogenarian founder and chairman of Occidental, a man of enormous wealth and power. Previously, Prince Charles had persuaded the Doctor to help Transglobe with fuel and I had met him on several occasions.

'I have never had a job outside the army,' I warned Dr Hammer. 'I know nothing about PR.'

This did not faze the Doctor. His attitude was that if I could persuade sponsors to part with £29 million worth of goods for Transglobe, I must know something about public relations.

When I told Ginnie the good news that our financial troubles were all over, as I had my first 'real job', she turned over in bed expressing the sincere hope that my new boss was not going to make a habit of calling me at 4am.

Later in the week I was flown to Los Angeles by private jet for an interview with the Doctor, who told me I was to consider myself his personal representative in Europe, not just one of his Occidental employees in London.

I explained that I already had a career in expeditions and would need, therefore, at least four months a year away from my Occidental desk. Surprisingly, this proved acceptable and I was given the job.

Within a month of the Doctor's call, I received another of equal significance. This was from Ollie Shepard, our old Transglobe friend, suggesting that we attempt what he described as 'the ultimate polar challenge', the grail of the international polar fraternity, to reach the North Pole with no outside support and no air contact. This was a journey long thought impossible but, with the advent of lightweight sledge materials and high-calorie light-weight foods, Oliver now believed it to be feasible.

'You can be the leader and I'll handle the cooking and science,' Ollie said. 'We will need to start organising at once.'

'Are you sure you want me to lead?' I asked him. 'After all it's your idea, your project.' Ollie gave a mock glance heavenwards. 'Think yourself lucky. Cooking and science are the difficult jobs.'

Left:

Prince Charles, Dr Hammer and a toy Bothie, watched by a young Jeremy Clarkson.

In a way he was right. Leading groups, large or small, was no real problem so long as you had a simple formula and stuck to it.

We agreed to overwinter at Ward Hunt Island, the most northerly point of Ellesmere Island, at the end of 1986, in readiness for a late February 1987 departure for the Pole.

Meanwhile I learned the ropes of a PR executive and office commuter in Victoria. I purchased a pinstripe suit, some striped shirts and six relatively daring ties. One of my responsibilities was to keep in favour with all the influential writers of the energy press who dealt with the world of petroleum. This entailed endless luncheons at expensive restaurants and the occasional evening outing to Stringfellow's nightclub. The idea was to nurture and maintain an unspoken *quid pro quo* relationship with these reporters so that they only said nice things about Occidental.

A few years later one of our North Sea oil platforms, Piper Alpha, blew up due to a gas explosion and over 160 employees were killed. The merciless media attack on Occidental which immediately ensued, made me doubt the value of the luncheons-and-Stringfellow's policy.

Other jobs included arranging and recording meetings, often at short notice, with Prince Charles, Mrs Thatcher, President Mitterrand's wife, Ted Heath, Robert Maxwell (car and turboprop projects), and numerous captains of European industry.

I was also tasked with selling the sprawling Occidental oil refinery site at Canvey Island to any buyer I could find, helping to arrange for the ex-king of Afghanistan to get back his throne, and raising huge sums of money for certain UK-based charities by various means. I was as successful at this last job as I was a complete failure at the first two.

I had to sue various magazines and newspapers who told libellous untruths about Dr Hammer (including *Private Eye* more than once), and purchase millions of dollars' worth of paintings at Christie's for the Doctor's art collections.

Right: Hauling sledges up a pressure ridge.

Many wealthy Americans believed Dr Hammer was a closet Communist, possibly in touch with the KGB, partly because his father had been the founder of the American Communist Party. In reality, he was the ultimate capitalist wheeler-dealer, albeit one who loved all things Russian, and the eight years I spent as his European consultant were an Aladdin's cave of experiences for me, an introduction to a world of high-fliers, big money and preposterous debts that I had never so much as sniffed in my narrow world of expeditions.

The Occidental work gave Ginnie and me a wonderful financial breather, for I was receiving a predictable and substantial income for the first time. But there can be few better moral tales in life than that of the foolish virgins. When times are good then that is the time to save up for the lean years ahead. I did not need reminding that I was on the wrong side of forty. Creaking bones and arthritic pains made me increasingly aware that I must maintain the impetus of the expeditions, the books and the lectures, without a break, since I could not rely on continuing employment with Dr Hammer (who consistently refused to give me a consultancy contract for more than one year at a time).

With this in mind, I spent as much time as possible preparing with

Oliver Shepard for the unsupported attempt on the North Pole. I would love to say that these preparations took place out of working hours, but the truth is that 90 per cent of them emanated from my Occidental PR desk. As long as I carried out what he asked, quickly and efficiently, the good Doctor gave me a long rein, so given a mile I took several inches, but took care not to overstep the mark.

I found difficulty obtaining a financial sponsor for the £70,000 we would need to pay for our flights to and from our proposed polar base. During one of the Doctor's London visits, he asked, 'What are you up to with those exhibitions of yours, Ran?'

Mike Stroud on a pressure ridge north of Ward Hunt Island.

'Expeditions, Doctor.'

'Yeah, exhibitions.'

'I'm trying to find a sponsor. It's very time-consuming.'

'Why didn't you say so?'

'Because I thought you might think I was angling to get sponsorship from you.'

The Doctor gave a throaty chuckle. 'You're dead right, I would . . . How much do you need and what would Occidental get in return?'

I told him and, a week later, he sent me a fax from LA in his dreadful handwriting agreeing to the sponsorship and with a PS adding, 'Now you can spend more time working for me and less time begging for dollars.'

Whenever I left my office I was aware there were other executives in Occidental who, naturally, coveted my job. The longer I spent abroad the greater the chance for one or other of them to impress the good Doctor, so that I would return to London to find my annual contract terminated.

Fortunately for me, Jan Milne, my Occidental PA, was an immensely capable, multilingual lady from Kent, both loyal and sharp-eyed. In any business where colleagues vie for promotion, you need eyes in the back of your head. With Jan firmly in place in the London office, I could go on expeditions without constantly having to look over my shoulder.

In the winter of 1986 Ollie and I joined Laurence (Flo) and Morag (Mo) Howell, the two best polar radio communicators in the business, on a ski-plane to remote Ward Hunt Island. A year before, Ginnie had dropped in at the island on a polar science sortie and taken the measurements of the steel framework of a burnt-out shack. This and three other hut skeletons had been abandoned there by a scientific project many years before.

The hut at Ward Hunt Island with Ginnie's made-to-measure Dayglo cover.

Ollie dropped me off with a television producer, Ginnie's pre-measured hut canvas, shovels, tools and one box of rations.

'I'll be back in twenty-four hours,' he shouted from the co-pilot's seat, 'with the rest of the food and kit.'

We erected the hut's cover, dug the place clear of snowdrifts, started a cooker and, very hungry, tore open the single ration box. Ollie, who has a severe squint, had given us the wrong box number. This was not a general rations pack at all: it contained only eggs. A bad storm prevented Ollie's next flight arriving for eight days, by which time I had become an expert egg chef.

Ollie and I were left alone on Ward Hunt Island through that long dark winter. We completed a number of scientific research programmes, but most of the time was spent working out the best method of towing heavy loads over ice-rubble, including twenty-five-foot high walls.

The sledge design solution that we sought was chimera-like. Now we had it, now we didn't. How best to tow a heavy weight over rough ice? Were solid towing-traces better than towing with ropes? Was it necessary to have amphibious sledges so we could paddle them through open water stretches? Or, could we dispense with the extra weight of float-bags and count on always being able to find a way round water zones?

We had brought many alternative items of gear, such as four types of tent. Which would do the best job with the least weight and bulk?

We made copious notes on our experiments, many modifications and many cold, dark trips to the pressure ridges north of our island.

There was little previous data for us to go on, because the world record

for unsupported northerly travel, set seventeen years before, was but ninety-eight miles north from land. This distance had been achieved by a three-person group led by the Scotsman Dr Hugh Simpson. Since then, nobody from any country, not even the Norwegians, had approached this distance, which remained the then world record. The following year, in late March, Ollie and I were almost ready to set out from Ward Hunt Island when a message arrived from Beefeater's in

Outside the Ward Hunt hut at sunrise.

London (the gin company which employed Ollie). Either he return within a week or he would lose his job. With a wife and home to look after the latter course was no option, so the Howells signalled for a ski-plane to remove him.

This was a body-blow to our carefully laid plans. We worked well together. Over two winters, and in conjunction with British Aerospace designer Steve Holland, we had gradually formulated a unique, amphibious,

Mike Stroud on thin ice. We had many unscheduled swims after being over-optimistic about the ice's strength.

sledge design and settled on a fifty-five-day ration/fuel load as being optimal for the Pole dash. Before he left Ollie agreed that I should use what was left of the short, polar travel season to mount an attempt. But who would replace him?

Flo and Mo made radio contact with Ginnie, who began a search at once for somebody who had recently undergone polar acclimatisation and was fresh from a man-haul journey. She found just such a person, Dr Mike Stroud, working in the Emergency Unit of Guy's Hospital. He agreed to fly out to join us and arrived at Ward Hunt Island four days later. Two days after that, on 1 April, the two of us left Mo and Flo at the hut and set out for the north.

Each of us towed 380lb. Three weeks later we passed the ninety-eight-mile point of the previous world record, but one of my toes, frostbitten after an unscheduled swim, became gangrenous. Back in London Mike arranged for a skin graft from my thigh to the frostbitten toe and we agreed to try again the next year, starting a month earlier. On all my previous expeditions I had gone to considerable lengths to carefully vet every team member, but this time, through force of circumstance, had taken on Mike sight unseen. That we proved compatible was remarkably lucky. There was no strained atmosphere, no hint of tension, not even the occasional heated exchange.

RF and Dmitry Shparo in 1990.

During our next attempt, ice conditions were about as bad as they could be and we failed to improve on the world record that we ourselves had set. So, a year later, in the spring of 1990, Mo and Flo joined Mike and me on a Soviet Air Force flight from Moscow to the Siberian mining town of Vorkuta.

Why this switch to the Soviet Arctic? My reasons were straightforward. Working for Dr Hammer, I had presented Raisa Gorbachev in Moscow with a magnificent porcelain figurine symbolising Soviet–American friendship. At our meeting I was impressed by her genuine friendliness and assumed her husband might be equally genuine in his ongoing overtures to the West.

I wrote to him to ask if we might try for the Pole from the Siberian coast. No previous Western outfit had ever made this request, either because the Pole was at least 100 miles further away than it was from Ward Hunt Island, or simply because they assumed the Soviets would turn them down.

**The Howells,
Mike Stroud and
RF unload
expedition gear at
Vorkuta, Siberia.**

Waiting for a new

lead to freeze over.

To my surprise Mr Gorbachev agreed to my proposal providing an approved Soviet citizen became our 'organiser' in Russia. A famous Russian polar explorer, Dr Dmitry Shparo, Hero of the Soviet Union, took on this task with great efficiency and accompanied the four of us all the way to Cape Arktikiski, our start point and the most northern point of land on Novya Zemlya.

This time our sledge loads were down to only 300lb each. Mike's diary recorded: 'The terrain consisted of broken, moving ice, a fragile skin on an ocean more than three thousand metres deep. On the seventh day my ski binding broke and I was condemned to wade through knee or thigh-high snow. We carried no spare bindings for every extra pound was at the expense of fuel or food for a journey that would entail cold and hunger.

'Despite my handicap we made good progress for a week and even when a three-day blizzard broke up the pack with winds in excess of ninety-five kilometres per hour we continued to travel, stumbling through the white-out and cursing the horizontally flung pellets of ice that filled our hoods and stung our eyes. We knew that if we became separated we would never find each other again. The man without the tent would die. Visibility was down to a couple of metres, footsteps were covered up as soon as they were made and shouts were immediately lost in the storm.

'After three weeks we were hindered by numerous areas of open water. It was slow work to lash our sledges together since our hands were clumsy in their frozen mitts. Any time lost through water-crossing delays was made up at the end of the day but the resulting thirteen- or fourteen-hour shifts took their toll and we began to have a serious weight problem.

'We each consumed 5,000 calories daily, yet after fifty days, we looked emaciated, having lost some 30lb each. Our resistance to cold had fallen away. Earlier, at minus 50°C, we had easily erected the tent poles by slipping off our mitts for brief periods. Now, even in the relative warmth of minus 20°C, our hands were extremely painful following the briefest loss of circulation.'

Mike Stroud on a newly frozen lead.

A hundred miles out we came across the fresh prints of a polar bear. I automatically felt for my revolver, only to realise we no longer had any form of defence as we had opted instead to save weight. For the first time on the Arctic pack ice I began to feel distinctly ill-at-ease. But exhaustion and hunger soon drove away fear. A large blister on the Achilles tendon had turned into a deep ulcer that was eating into my heel. Even on skis I needed to limp to favour the wound. My eyesight had begun to blur and my pupils increasingly refused to focus. After a previous expedition five years before, an eye surgeon had warned me to stay clear of bright sunshine as I risked losing my sight but, because of the unavoidable fogging of goggles, I often navigated without eye protection.

I looked back on one occasion and there was no sign of Mike in all the dazzling white expanse of moving ice. Something made me take the unusual step of retracing my tracks. I heard him calling and moved faster. I found him swimming in a narrow canal with sheer, five-foot-high ice banks. Only his head was above water and the air temperature was minus 42°C. He wore a heavy backpack and his mitts were encumbered by the frozen, leather straps of his ski sticks. I managed to pull him out, but only just. Somehow we put the tent up and fired the cooker.

Mike outside our tent, cleaning the cooker.

Over the following weeks we both fell in six or seven times, sometimes because of weak canal banks, but also through misjudging weak ice. Had we both fallen in at the same time the outcome would have been quick and fatal.

Around 88° North, with 720 kilometres behind us, our strength quite suddenly disappeared as the extreme loss of body weight reached the point where we became debilitated. Cold began to pervade our bodies, and sleep, always difficult on ice that shrieks and shudders, became well nigh impossible when we had to lie on thinly padded bones. In addition, my eyesight became too poor to navigate, so I took to following close behind the vague outline of Mike's body, cursing each time I tripped over unseen ice blocks.

On the forty-eighth day, by which time we were within a tantalising eighty-nine miles of the Pole, I began to feel the icy north wind blowing on to my right ear rather than my nose, indicating a change of course. After an hour of this I tapped my ski stick against Mike's back intending to query his compass bearing. I discovered that he was dazed and could hardly speak. With no idea of direction he was simply plodding on in a hypoglycaemic trance, his body crying out for an energy source to stimulate his dangerously flagging metabolic rate.

We were ten days away from the Pole, having lost twelve or fourteen days through the contrary drift and the broken ski binding, when we ran out of food. The surface conditions in the Arctic that year were as good as or better than in 1986, so we would in fact have been better off back on the Canadian side. But this we could not have known in advance.

We activated a miniature radio beacon as arranged with Dmitry, and within twenty-four hours a Soviet gunship helicopter took off from an ice island 300 miles to the north-east. The next eight days we remained on their ice floe during a major break-up, which split their airstrip into seven floes and their hut camp into two.

Because my feet were very swollen, Mike gave me desiccation tablets, which had the unforeseen result of shifting a kidney stone in my urinary tract. I was violently sick and contorted with stomach pains.

A week later we returned to Moscow, where the Soviet Komsomol President gave us medals and Dmitry Shparo confirmed that we had made the longest and fastest unsupported journey in the Arctic to date. Our furthest point north now stood at over 300 miles nearer the Pole than the previous world record. We knew we could refine our system the following spring to complete the last eighty-nine miles, less than one degree, to the Pole itself. The question was whether someone else would beat us to the goal that our group had worked so long and so hard to achieve. The answer was not long in coming. Back in our usual hunting ground of the Ward Hunt route to the Pole, three Norwegians, led by the superb cross-country skier Erling Kagge, had reached the Pole and, as we

With Mike on the edge of the Arctic Ocean.

returned to London, they announced their 'unsupported' claim to the world's press.

This was a great surprise, or rather shock, to Mike and me because, halfway through our own journey, Flo had sent us a radio report confirming that, 'The Norwegian team's attempt at an unsupported trip is over because one of the three was removed yesterday by ski-plane with frostbite.'

There had already been a number of expedition groups, mainly Russian, which had made it to the Pole, but had made no unsupported claims because they acknowledged the unwritten rules of the international polar fraternity. These rules may appear very stringent to the outsider and the media can make them appear petty but, if you have travelled to the Pole yourself, you will not think them so. Let me give one example.

In 1988 Colonel Vladimir Chukov of the Soviet Special Forces led an unsupported Pole attempt with a team of eight. Two of his men died in the attempt and two became so weak that a helicopter evacuated them along with the corpses. Chukov and his remaining men later reached the Pole without further support, but they knew the rules and accepted that their earlier brief air contact had compromised their claim.

So what exactly does 'unsupported' mean? Most Russian, Canadian and British polar travellers agree that every member of a group that sets out from the coastline must reach the Pole with no contact en route with any human or any outside sourced supplies not carried by the team. Motive power must be purely manual.

This means that, if a team member drops out en route for any reason, the whole team is disqualified or, to use a friendlier word, compromised. If there had been a third man with Mike and I when, for instance, Mike's binding broke (which alone may easily have made the difference between success and failure), then that man could have given Mike his binding and either made his own way back to land or

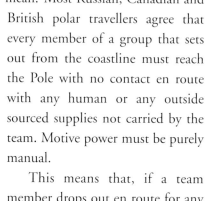

Left:
RF negotiating an
ice-rubble belt.

Opposite:
Mike Stroud on
an old ice floe.

'This cruel land can cast a spell
which no temperate clime can match'

T. E. LAWRENCE

6

BLINDED BY SCIENCE

T. E. Lawrence (of Arabia) trained as an archaeologist at Oxford and determined to unearth the site of the mythical Ubar, the last lost city in Arabia marked on Ptolemy's famous first map of the world but, unlike Petra, not yet identified. Lawrence dubbed the place the 'Atlantis of the Sands', but he was killed shortly before he was due to lead an expedition to discover its whereabouts.

When fighting the Marxists in Dhofar I heard the *bedu* talk of Irem, their name for Ubar, and I determined to find it. My guide told me, 'Irem was the finest city in all Arabia, built like Paradise but destroyed by God.'

Since the dawn of civilisation the keystone of trade between the Phoenician and Muscat sailors was frankincense, which came only from the incense orchards of Dhofar and which for two thousand years was more valuable even than gold. Ubar was the desert watering place from which great caravans of two thousand camels and five hundred men set out on their journey through the Empty Quarter to service the incense markets of the world. On Ptolemy's AD 150 map no cities are shown in Arabia's south-eastern deserts save for Omanum Emporum, the market of Oman, known to later writers, travellers and the Koran as Ubar, or Irem, city of the lost people of Ad.

RF and a Sultanate soldier during a reconnaissance for the lost city of Ubar.

The Book of Genesis indicates that Ad settled his tribe between the Empty Quarter and the Indian Ocean.

Until 1969 the Sultan had allowed only two expeditions to search for Ubar and neither had been successful. In 1930 Bertram Thomas, the Sultan's financial adviser, completed a remarkable 900-mile camel journey during which he came across 'well-worn tracks, a hundred yards across and graven into the Plain'. One of his guides told him, 'Look, there is the road to Ubar.'

Using Thomas's data in 1953 the US archaeologist Dr Wendell Phillips travelled to the Sands of Mitan and relocated Thomas's well-worn tracks to nowhere. Fifteen years later I mounted my own first Ubar search using two of my platoon's Land Rovers and aiming for the Wadi Mitan. I had with me a quote from Phillips summarising his failed search: 'The mystery of Ubar remains unsolved. In a completely inaccessible area where today there is little or no camel traffic, a well-marked highway centuries old, made by thousands of camel caravans, leads west for many miles from the famous spice lands of Dhofar and then, on a bearing of N 75° W mysteriously disappears without a trace in the great sands. A dozen Ubars could well be lost among these high dunes, unknown even to the present-day *bedu*. I firmly believe some day some explorer will solve the mystery of Ubar, Arabia's most intriguing lost city.'

Close to the Saudi–Yemeni border in the Empty Quarter. A midday halt.

I knew that my then boss, the Sultan, would not approve of my not very military Ubar sortie using his vehicles and troops in the opposite direction to that of our Marxist foe. Consequently I had to be careful not to break down in the sand dunes needing to radio the Sultan's only Beaver aircraft to drop me spare parts. I took no guide, the two Land Rovers and seven men.

For two days we struggled through the soft sands between Qafa and the Wadi Atinah. By the time we reached the then uninhabited site of today's

One of the Ubar
Expedition
Discovery vehicles
negotiating soft
sand furrows.

Fasad camp, we had burst two tyres and broken one half-shaft. We travelled thence, using the sun and the passage of time, as due west as the land allowed and came to a place of a dozen well-trodden camel trails.

'Very old,' my men all observed. But they knew I was looking for 'old trails' and they liked me to be happy. So, I did not trust their judgement. On the fourth day we broke our last spare half-shaft and dined with a lone family of Rashidi camel herders in the dunes. They gave us fresh, frothy camel's milk. We left them water and flour. They knew a man in the Wadi Jadileh, two camel-days west, who would 'have news of Irem'. We made it to the Jadileh but saw nobody in the whole vast, shimmering, desert landscape.

From this first failed sortie I learned never to try again without a guide and to double my stock of spare half-shafts.

The best desert guide, Sheikh Nashran bin Sultan, was keen to help but, of course, did not know the exact location of Ubar. Nobody did. But he might know *bedu* who had seen ruins, pillars maybe, in the sands. I tried to narrow down the search area near the Wadi Mitan.

'Which side of the Saudi–Yemeni–Omani border is it?' I asked.

'Where are these borders you talk about?' Nashran asked. 'Are they marked with posts?'

'There are no markers.' I told him what he already knew.

'Ubar likewise.' He smiled his superior *bedu* smile. 'Forget the borders. We must look for Rashidi in the sands.'

We did find Rashidi who had lived their entire lives in the area most likely to house Ubar, but none knew of any likely site. For many days we drove into the dunes in the area of Thomas's 'tracks' sighting. We searched high and low until called back to operational work by my sergeant.

Aerial view of Shis'r fort in 1968.

Over the next six years I mounted three further attempts to locate Ubar and all failed despite many false alarms and raised hopes usually resulting from *bedu* who swore blind they had seen ruins but, when they led us to the spot, professed profound surprise that there was nothing to be seen.

The obvious answer was to search for the city by air but, throughout the

Opposite: Nick Clapp, NASA scientist Ron Blom and RF consult a satellite map in dune country.

A graveyard on
the edge of
Salalah Plain,
1991. We searched
many such sites
for Ubar clues.

1980s, I kept postponing the project on the grounds that nobody else was searching for Ubar, whereas several rival groups were all keen to be the first to reach the North Pole unsupported.

In the summer of 1990, recovered from the rigours of our record-setting Soviet journey, I focused anew on Ubar and spent a week in Muscat raising the necessary funds and supplies from old Omani friends and expatriate retailers. An American colleague from Occidental Oil Oman agreed to $20,000 worth of support; BP promised unlimited fuel; and one sheikh, Mohammed Darwish, agreed to loan me Land Rover Discovery vehicles, which I knew from past journeys were far better for long periods in soft sand than any of their competitors. The Sultan of Oman also agreed to help and gave orders to the Royal Oman Police to provide helicopter support as needed.

I decided to complete a reconnaissance journey immediately, in readiness for a fully fledged archaeological search the following year.

I had agreed with an old film director friend from Los Angeles, Nick Clapp, to run the expedition on a two-prong basis. I would organise the administration, Oman liaison and lead the expedition in the field, and he would be responsible for filming the entire project. The theme of his film would be the search for Ubar and he would select a volunteer group of American archaeologists to excavate likely sites as soon as we located them.

Nick had worked for a year editing the film made by Dr Hammer of the Transglobe expedition. We had become friends and he knew about my Arabian experiences. A subsequent three-day visit to Oman to film the golden oryx had fired him with enthusiasm to film a documentary there and the Ubar search gave him a suitable theme.

Right: Andy Dunsire and RF descend into a well at the mouth of the Wadi Naheez during the search for Ubar.

Unfortunately for Nick, he and his Los Angeles fund-raiser friends were unable to raise any funds and stood no chance at all of obtaining Sultanate permission to film in Dhofar. Together, however, we stood a good chance of achieving our aims.

Following the example of another lost-city searcher, Nick made contact with NASA to request that the Shuttle crew photograph the Ubar search area from space using teledetection systems to highlight potential sites of the lost city. NASA promised to do their best and, in due course, produced a satellite image clearly showing 'well-worn tracks' as well as a nearby L-shaped site, which looked man-made. Nick was thrilled. He also found a suitable archaeologist, Dr Juris Zarins, with many years of Arabian experience.

We all met up in Dhofar and the reconnaissance of the L-shaped site got under way. Juris Zarins was singularly unimpressed by this NASA location. Different surface patterns and the movement of the sand had shaped a letter 'L' between two separate dune formations. The great NASA find was merely an ancient lake bed, so we were back at square one.

By hoping for space-age technology to identify the actual site of Ubar, I had fallen into the trap of suggesting as much to the Sultan and to the sponsors. I had known that the glamorous mix of satellites and buried cities would excite even the most reluctant sponsor. Now, with our space card a busted flush, I still had to convince the Sultan and our sponsors to back the main expedition.

Over the week that remained of our permitted stay in Oman, we had to

come up with something new, some rationale to keep our search on the rails. I hotted up the search using a helicopter to take us to any remote sites where Ubar might conceivably be. Most of these places were the result of stories told to Major Trevor Henry, the Sultan's last remaining British intelligence officer in Dhofar. Trevor, a tough and enigmatic Scot, had been my sergeant instructor fifteen years before in a long jungle-warfare course in Brunei. He had fought in the Dhofar war, stayed on when peace came and knew more about the country and its people than any European alive.

Trevor had completed land patrols to or flights over all the sites I had queried, whether NASA-identified or *bedu*-rumoured. He had seen nothing of relevance and told me, 'If the city is out there

Andy Dunsire and RF in the Tawi Ateer river system.

at all, it has to be sub-surface.' Our whirlwind tour included every known archaeological site in southern Oman that was involved with the frankincense trade.

My resulting report summarising the reconnaissance journey was sent to the Sultan, the relevant Omani ministries and to all our sponsors. It made the most of a bad job by stating a few arcane historical facts, theorising a good deal out of very little and drawing out the scarce clues that we had put together from Juris's few finds. These included some Bronze Age ceramics he had found at Shis'r, the site of a small Sultanate fort on the southern rim of the Empty Quarter. He had gone so far as to theorise, 'It is not impossible that Shis'r may turn out to be the mythical Ubar.'

Although he had written this to help the report, Juris knew that the reconnaissance had actually proved nothing at all, and he was as surprised as I was when, some months later, the Sultan gave me permission to proceed with the main expedition the following autumn.

We set out in November 1991 and drove three Land Rover Discoverys five hundred miles south from Muscat to Salalah, where I visited the Governor of Dhofar. He gave me permission to excavate any or all of the eleven sites I had listed for him and also for our team to be based in Shis'r where, he proudly informed me, his government had just built ten houses and a mosque for the local *bedu*.

From Shis'r, over the next two months, our searches and our surface digs covered much of Dhofar from the Indian Ocean to the northern sands. In our search for clues we swam underground rivers, descended deep pits and limestone karsts, scraped at burial mounds and frankincense storage vats, wandered numerous desert sites deep in the

dunes and photographed ancient cave paintings. Juris was in seventh heaven, since this whole country was to him an archaeological treasure-house and he was the only archaeologist allowed therein by the Sultan.

The stone wall above the cleft at Shis'r, 1991.

Nick was also deliriously happy, producing his documentary of a seldom-filmed, remote and fascinating land. Unlike Juris and Nick, I was decidedly unhappy, because this expedition was proving no more successful at lost-city finding than my previous six attempts over the last twenty-three years.

The dig. There was
a pile of rubble
close by the cliff
which jutted over
the original water
hole of Shis'r,
rubble which a
previous French
archaeologist
acquaintance of
Juris had once
looked at and
logged as mere
sixteenth-century
remains.

Hi-tech satellite images had not worked and now traditional searching was faring no better. Although I hate to admit it, our big break, when it came, arrived not through deduction or cleverness but through sheer good luck. Or possibly the will of Allah.

Three days before Christmas, shading behind a wall in Shis'r, I was discussing communications problems with Ginnie, who was in Dhofar to set up our HF radio systems. In the heat of the midday sun we both fell asleep and I awoke to hear a heated discussion on the other side of the wall between two Omanis. I recognised their voices. Both were liaison staff from the Ministry of Heritage, whose job was to keep tabs on our activities and report back to their minister. He, in turn, would report to the Sultan.

Their conversation was deeply disturbing. For two weeks they had observed Nick and his team busily filming everything everywhere, although not one archaeological trowel had been raised in earnest. They knew that Juris Zarins and his team of young archaeology students were in Shis'r with all the necessary equipment to hand. So why no digging? It seemed as though archaeology was merely our front, just an excuse to gain coveted permission to make a film of Dhofar generally.

Since the working title of Nick's film was *The Search for Ubar*, it clearly did not really matter much to him whether or not we actually ever located the city. The act of searching was enough to warrant a fascinating film. The two Omanis on whom I had eavesdropped had a good point, and I saw big trouble ahead when they made their next report to their minister. There was no time to be lost, so I went straight to Juris. I told him that we were in trouble and he must start digging at once.

'Where?' Juris tilted his Indiana Jones hat back. 'Dhofar is a big place.'

'Anywhere you like,' I begged him. 'Just get digging and make sure the ministry guys see you at it.'

There was a pile of rubble close by the cliff which jutted over the

Right: RF helping the archaeologists at Shis'r. The pickaxe was removed and replaced with a small brush.

A burial chamber
found by Juris
Zarins close to the
Shis'r site.

original water hole of Shis'r, rubble which a previous French archaeologist acquaintance of Juris had once looked at and logged as mere sixteenth-century remains, useless in terms of Ubar chronology. However, to dig around existing rubble was a far less pointless exercise than excavating in the middle of nowhere, Juris's only alternative.

So, two days before Christmas, with a workforce of four Omanis, three Asians and six Americans, Juris began his methodical attack on the Shis'r rubble in order to allay the suspicions of the local KGB.

After that everything happened in a rush. Within a week the outline of the rubble heap had taken on the clear-cut silhouette of a ruined tower connected by low battlements to a second round tower and a beautifully built horseshoe tower to its east. Pottery and flints were unearthed hourly including, to Juris's great pleasure, both Greek and Roman-style urns from the period that would have been Ubar's heyday.

Days later a piece of red pottery was found identical to a unique style found in Uruq, Mesopotamia. This find alone pre-dated previous thinking as to the commencement of trade between Mesopotamia and south Arabia from 5,000 to 4,000 BC. 'This find,' Juris told me, 'could well have a profound effect on many of our evolving theories about the whole history of this area.'

Ginnie and I spent many hours over the next month plodding about in the desert, six or seven miles east of Shis'r, searching for subsidiary sites rich in axe heads. Once, when this area was less arid, according to Juris, travellers would have camped within sight of the many-towered citadel of Shis'r or Ubar, but far enough away to settle their camels and sort out their loads. Altogether we found thirty-

The soapstone chess pieces found at Shis'r.

five such camp sites to the north, west and east of the citadel and up to eight miles away from it.

For 900 kilometres of desert in every direction there was no archaeological site with any edifice even a quarter of the size of Shis'r's Ubar. The Ubar towers would have been easily visible from twenty kilometres away.

Some of the rooms the team uncovered in our second month at Shis'r yielded rich finds covering the entire period from the second millennium BC

until around AD 300, when trading activities seemed to have dropped off. The finds included six soapstone chess pieces, three inches high, part of the only chess set ever unearthed in Arabia and well over a thousand years old. One axehead was 250,000 years old.

Early in February, I officially handed over to Dhofar's Field Director for Archaeology all our thousands of carefully logged and tagged artefacts from the Ubar dig.

On 5 February 1992, an article by John Noble Wilford was splashed across the front page of the *New York Times* giving the news of our Ubar discovery. This was picked up and given wide coverage around the world. All major newspapers and TV networks across the USA gave the story prime rating and suggested that the project was an entirely American-inspired success. 'Guided by ancient maps and sharp-eyed surveys from space,' Wilford eulogised, 'archaeologists and explorers have discovered a lost city deep in the sands of Arabia.' All successive articles and TV films on the topic stated that NASA space technology had led to the finding of Ubar.

Juris Zarins did his best to be kind about these reports by saying, 'It sounds as though space technology is at work and all that kind of rubbish. That's not entirely true but it sounds good. The truth is we found the city by hard work and excavation. The satellite imagery allowed us to eliminate sites so we could concentrate on the most probable areas.'

Nick Clapp himself began to believe in the 'NASA found it' claptrap. Certainly, this gave his film a wonderful 'ancient and modern' angle. If NASA had in any way led us to believe that Shis'r was Ubar, Professor Juris Zarins would never have said, as he did in March 1992, 'I had never thought that Shis'r was Ubar even when we started to dig.'

I would like to establish the facts rather than the NASA spin, but it is an uphill struggle because the scientific community has already begun, in their learned magazines, to perpetuate the Wilford myth, which is a gross distortion of the truth.

The actual facts of our discovery can best be summarised by openly admitting that a large slice of luck, a good deal of hard work and the experience-honed instincts of Juris were responsible. The NASA satellite imagery located nothing at all other than the L-shaped site, which proved illusory, and a number of desert tracks, full details of which were already well known.

RF and Ginnie at a camp in the dunes. The sun yet to burn off the nighttime chill.

Professor Mohammed Bakalla of King Saud University, a noted scholar of Arab history, wrote, 'Your discovery is important and I expect future discovery will unveil the extraordinary civilisation of Irem and Ad's nation cities underneath or close by.'

Five weeks after reporting our first Shis'r finding to the Sultan of Oman, he flew me by helicopter to his Muscat palace. He was delighted with the success of the expedition and keen to ensure continued excavation at Shis'r until the ruins were fully revealed.

'It is definitely Ubar?' he asked me.

'I believe so, Your Majesty. It is difficult to know what else it could be.'

The subsequent UNESCO report on the excavation summarised: 'The purely archaeological discoveries that are emerging from Shis'r are of the greatest importance for South Arabia in their own right . . . The archaeological integrity of the site should not be affected by possible disputes regarding its name.'

Despite this acclaim, I made the mistake of racing back from Oman for a business meeting. This proved to be a bad mistake, as I missed the press conferences which Nick Clapp held both in Muscat and, later, in the United States. As a result the entire expedition was presented as an American project organised and led by Americans using NASA technology.

Too late I tried to alert the media to the truth, but the damage was done. My literary agent, Ed Victor (George Greenfield had retired), shook his head disbelievingly. 'I thought you were an old hand, Ran, but you have allowed yourself to be a sucker twice over.'

He explained. 'Number one. Where big publicity and media folk are concerned you do not trust anyone, however friendly and honest you may think them. Number two. You plan your diary to ensure that you and you alone orchestrate such key events as press conferences about your own activities. You do not spend twenty-six years on and off searching for a fabulous lost city and achieve the unique success of finding it, only to miss out on announcing the fact to the world because you are too rushed. You have to be there

RF hands over the Ubar finds to the Minister for Antiquities.

in person with the press. You have to be quoted. Remember, possession is nine-tenths of the law. Unless you possess those microphones at the brief moment of glory, you can count your bottom dollar that your friends will grab that glory for themselves.'

Despite this ticking off, Ed proceeded to obtain for me an excellent contract for my book about my long Ubar search. Entitled *Atlantis of the Sands*, I wrote it during what proved to be my last four months of work at Occidental.◆

The Lessons Learned

Never set out into a great desert without a guide. Even though he may prove useless, you will never know this if you do not take him

◆

When hi-tech systems fail, be ready to revert immediately to traditional means of doing the job

◆

Where big publicity and the media are concerned, do not trust anyone, however friendly and honest you may think them

◆

Possession, at press conferences, is nine-tenths of the law. You must be there in person. You must be quoted. Otherwise you can count on others grabbing that key, short moment for their own ends

◆

'Endure what can't be mended'

ISAAC WATTS

7

LIVE DONKEY
OR DEAD LION

D r Hammer died in 1990, and although his successor did not renew my contract I continued to write letters to newspaper editors for years after his death to counteract the numerous lice that crawled from the woodwork to write malicious and denigrating books or articles about their former employer. Like vultures, they were keen to peck at the corpse now it could not bite back. I would love to have sued them silly but, sadly, the law allows the dead to be defamed with impunity.

So, after eight interesting years as a corporate gopher, I was back on my own and very thankful I had kept up the expedition work, the books and the lectures. The sudden loss of my excellent Occidental salary was, as a result, not too much of a jolt.

The Occidental income had enabled us to move out of London and Ginnie had started farming in Exmoor National Park. She bought five pedigree Aberdeen Angus cows and, gradually, taught herself the ropes until she was running one of the largest and most successful beef cattle farms in the south-west, despite the advent of BSE soon after she started up.

Although Ginnie could no longer participate in the expeditions, she supported them in every way possible and dealt with press enquiries when I

RF and Mike Stroud man-hauling 490lb sledge-loads.

was away. We both knew that the media can be as cruel as they can be kind, and a sharp reminder of this came in the shape of a feature article in the Canadian *Macleans* magazine. This painted me as a highly unsavoury character on numerous counts and the effect on potential sponsors of future expeditions in the Canadian Arctic was likely to be disastrous.

As a general rule I believe it best to try to ignore malign and libellous articles rather than exacerbate matters in the courts, but like every rule there are important exceptions. In this case the *Macleans* reporter in question had attacked me personally for seventeen years and was likely to continue if his teeth were not pulled. So we took his magazine to court. The only demonstrably inaccurate statement in his article that stood a chance of being nailed as libel, however, was the assertion that no expedition of mine was of scientific value.

Mike Stroud and Vivian Fuchs gave evidence of their involvement in our scientific research over the years and the twelve-person High Court jury unanimously awarded us damages of £100,000 and a full apology. An appeal reduced the damages to £10,000 but *Macleans* had to pay the considerable court costs, which would have broken Ginnie and me had we lost.

Mike Stroud contemplates the vast distances involved in our proposed crossing.

A year before Dr Hammer's death, Charlie Burton had summoned me to the Royal Geographical Society to study a proposal put together by him and Oliver Shepard to complete the first ever crossing of Antarctica on foot and without support.

I knew this had been tried by Russian and American groups using fuel-efficient vehicles but, to date, all attempts had failed. Too far, too high, too cold.

I told Ollie and Charlie, 'Since neither machines nor dog-teams can make it, humans man-hauling sledges are out of the question.' But the two of them showed me their plan and it seemed to make sense.

'Scott was dead right,' Charlie summarised. 'Manpower, not dogs, is the efficient method. Our journey will prove it.'

I researched previous attempts at unsupported man-haul journeys in

The forbidding
and potentially
deadly Antarctic
landscape.

Antarctica. An Anglo-Canadian group led by Briton Roger Mear had just managed, in seventy-five days, to make it as far as the Pole, but they were then airlifted out. Their attempt was the most successful journey to date, but Charlie's proposal involved twice the distance.

While involved in the Ubar search, I had made a few tentative moves to set up the Antarctic crossing attempt. Prince Charles had agreed to be its patron and suggested we use it to raise funds for multiple sclerosis. Back in 1990, at his behest, we had raised £2,300,000 and helped set up Europe's first MS research centre in Cambridge. A further major success would bolster the centre's achievements.

Our preparations progressed slowly until, in May 1991, one of Ollie's 'KGB informants in Norway' warned us that Erling Kagge, our most active polar rival at the time, was announcing to the Scandinavian media his intention to cross the Antarctic continent in 1992.

I knew Kagge was an exceptionally strong cross-country skier and speed with endurance were the keys to success in Antarctica. Neither Ollie nor Charlie, though 100 per cent dependable, were keen on pushing themselves to the limits. I decided to confront this issue at once and, explaining my Kagge worries, I suggested we ask the highly competitive Mike Stroud to join our team.

The ANI ski-plane, based at the Patriot Hills ice airstrip and camp.

Not long afterwards Ollie called to say he and Charlie had both decided to change their roles. 'We would want to enjoy the crossing,' he explained. 'Once you get competitive, any signs of enjoyment are tantamount to mutiny.' So, they took on the role of the organisers and Mike agreed to join the field team on the condition he would conduct an extensive physiological research programme throughout the journey.

The challenge that faced us involved very exact timing because the Antarctic travel season does not last long. We could not hope to set out before 1 November 1992 from the Atlantic coastline of Antarctica, and we must reach the US base of MacMurdo on the Pacific coast by 6.30am on 16 February 1993. Not a minute later, because at that precise time the very last ship of the year would leave Antarctica.

The mathematics were, therefore, very simple. We must each tow a start-out load of over 450lb, at least 16 miles a day, for 108 days. I knew this was a performance well in excess of any man-hauling achievement in history. Mike agreed that there was every likelihood that it was not physically possible.

Nonetheless, whatever business you are in, it is bad practice to allow your chief rival a clear run at a main prize without even mounting a challenge.

We flew with Morag Howell to Punta Arenas in southern Chile and waited there, as did Kagge, for two long weeks. Our hoped-for start date faded away, and with it our slim chances of success. We finally made the nine-hour flight to Antarctica in an ancient DC6, landing on a blue-ice airstrip, and then, switching our cargo immediately to a small ski-plane, flew on to our distant start point on Berkner Island. Only when we had waved goodbye to Morag and the pilot did the full impact of the task ahead sink in. This was just as well, since there was no temptation to jump back on board the Twin Otter.

The first 200 miles of our route from the coastline took us through largely uncharted crevasse zones. We were in trouble almost immediately.

A major problem was the weight of each sledge. Despite our best efforts to keep to only vital equipment (toothpaste and soap, for instance, were not taken since their absence would not threaten our survival for three months), each sledge weighed 485lb, by far the heaviest one-man sledge-load of any recorded expedition. The danger was not just the sheer difficulty of shifting them at all: as worrying was the heavy 'footprint' they would bring to bear on thin snow bridges over crevasses.

The maximum sledge-load known to have been pulled by a dog for up to 300 miles was 150lb. In 1903 Scott and Shackleton towed loads of 175lb each and, on his last fatal expedition, Scott towed 200lb. Reinhold Messner, the world's greatest mountain climber, wrote of a sledge he hauled in Antarctica: 'Two hundred and sixty four pounds is a load for a horse, not a human being.'

Ahead of us lay 1,700 miles and a huge climb to over 11,000 feet. We braced ourselves against our dog harnesses and found, to our immense relief, that we could just drag the sledges forward providing we applied maximum effort at every step. Any obstacle such as an eight-inch rut was enough to jam the front end of the runners.

RF en route to the edge of Antarctica, the starting-point for the crossing attempt.

We spent twenty-six days merely ascending the Filchner Ice Shelf before we even reached the edge of the actual landmass of Antarctica, the true start point of any attempt to cross the continent. The ice shelf was really only a mass of ice grounded on the sea-floor and temporarily attached to the continent. The constant seaward movement of its surface caused a highly lethal crevasse environment. We fell into a good many, but the safety ropes between us and our sledges saved us from death.

The sledge harnesses bit into our skin, muscle and tendons. So did our boots. Blisters began to form. The sun and wind started to crack our lips, despite preventative creams. I knew the pattern well. First my inner anger would be directed at the weather, the equipment and the ice. Later, at my companion. The same process would hold good for Mike.

On the first day we stopped, utterly exhausted, after five hours. We had managed four miles. Now we only had another 1,696 miles to go and, since we had food for one hundred days, there was still time to find a way of increasing our daily average to sixteen miles. If we did not do so, this daily average would itself quickly shoot up. We could not afford a single rest day, no matter what our health or the weather.

Our hands and feet began to blister and become poisoned. We took

antibiotics, but there was a limited supply. The skins on our skis loosened and needed constant adjustment with cold, cracked fingers. Our eyes hurt and we sometimes needed to take off our goggles when they froze up. Mike had to keep his off one day in white-out conditions and, that night, suffered the agony of sun-blindness. Amethocaine drops eventually sorted him out.

Throughout the three-month journey, we both remained fearful of crevasses. As with anti-personnel mines in a war zone, you only know you have trodden on one when it is too late. I remembered a cynical journalist in London, on Radio 4, telling his listeners, 'Of course, it's not the same now as it was eighty years ago with Scott. Now you have all the trappings of modern technology.'

I could think of no 'trapping' which could prevent us falling into crevasses, stop us slowly starving (as we were at a daily deficiency of 2,000 calories input over output), nor stop us feeling excessively cold.

Mike's diary entries included: 'Gaping holes left and right, a few yards away in the gloom . . . nerve-wracking . . . the bridges are soft and difficult.'

Unnamed Antarctic mountains.

Opposite: A typical Antarctic crevasse. Throughout the three-month journey, we both remained fearful of crevasses at all times. There were many narrow escapes.

On one occasion, in a thick mist, Mike fell twenty feet into a crevasse, landing on a ledge above a drop with no visible bottom. His heavy sledge, an aerial torpedo, thankfully missed him but struck the crevasse wall and shattered in two. We were blessed with good fortune, since the vital runners were not damaged so repairs were easy.

Our two petrol cookers suffered from leakage problems round the washers and caused a number of fires in the tent during the journey. We repaired much broken gear using our penknives, tweezers and metal cut from empty fuel bottles.

We progressed to nine-hour travel days, but still averaged only ten miles. We needed to get rid of weight now in time to make mileage early enough to keep the target feasible. The time to take hard decisions comes early on, and we did so by burying our extra warm clothes. We knew they would be vital as we climbed higher and temperatures plummeted. Maybe we would have second thoughts later. But there would be no 'later' if we could not get a move on now. So the clothes were sacrificed.

At some point a mile or so west of the island, we were hauling through a disturbed ice zone when a phenomenon occurred which I have never heard talked of or written about before or since. The ice-shelf entered a hyperactive

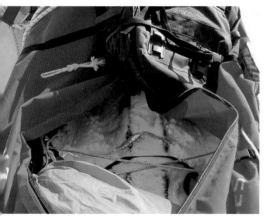

phase for no apparent reason, causing hitherto 'safe' snow bridges to collapse into the great crevasses that laced the entire feature. And we were caught in the middle. Each sudden implosion was accompanied by a thunderous roar and clouds of snow vapour rising high in the air, as if from a geyser. One gaping hole, which opened up a mere ten paces ahead of Mike, was 45 feet wide by 120 feet in length, and lay directly across our intended route.

All around us new explosions announced further craters. We must escape to a safer area. But where was safer? At any moment we expected to be plunged into an abyss. We headed towards the distant hump of Berkner Island as fast as we could move. Time stood still. For an hour our luck held. One immense crater appeared immediately between Mike and me. One moment there was solid ice ahead of me, the next Mike's ski trail had vanished and the roar of imploding snow dropping into the bowels of the ice-shelf boomed up in successive echoing waves from the blue pit into which drooped the safety rope that joined us. Late that night we reached Berkner's and camped on solid ice with a luxurious feeling of safety.

Left: Mike's broken sledge after his crevasse accident. The hull was cracked across its entire width, and was held together for the remaining 1,200 miles by the runners alone.

Mike Stroud

on blue ice

somewhere in

Antarctica.

Dr Mike Stroud watches as RF balances on the miniature weighing-scales. At the South Pole we found a slab of plywood which provided a solid base for the scales; vital for Mike's physiological research programme.

South Pole. We had man-hauled 700 miles and felt as though we had come to the end of our tether.

Our Norwegian rival Kagge had altered his original plan to cross Antarctica to an attempt to reach the Pole solo and unsupported. This he had done. With a sledge half the weight of our own, he had arrived ten days before us and achieved a world record.

Somehow our admiration for his great skiing ability and strength, even the mere fact that he was from Norway – a country of 'polar gods' in the minds of most polar Britons – gave us an additional concern. If he had halted at the Pole, he must have good reason for doing so. He must have known it would be stupid to continue.

Our problem was that of putting Norwegians on a pedestal and feeling inferior. I can remember having created the same illusion when in the Arab army. Then I had begun to believe that all Marxist terrorists were invincible. The danger is a loss of self-belief, of the confidence necessary to keep battling on.

There is also, of course, the danger of blindly determining to keep going at all costs instead of recognising the need to turn back – to fail but to live to fight another day.

Scott made the South Pole but died on his way back to base having exhausted his supplies, whereas Shackleton, a few years before, turned back just before reaching the Pole and, as a result, just made it back alive to his ship. His policy was 'better a live donkey than a dead lion'.

We spent one hour in our tent at the Pole and then continued. All our previous sufferings were as nothing compared with the days which followed the Pole. The wind blew at force five, day after day, and the January temperatures dropped steadily.

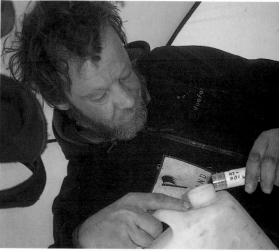

Mike pouring a blood sample into a storage container.

Two days from the Pole, Mike lanced my foot in several places to release quantities of poison, and I felt much better for a while. I applied haemorrhoid cream to various parts including the raw regions of my crotch, scabbed lips, nose and chin. Diarrhoea attacks came often, which reopened the haemorrhoids and made any leg movement miserable. Mike diagnosed 'deep-seated infection in the foot bone'. At night the pain was difficult to bear in silence. By day the rigid ski boots worked against the damaged areas and I learned the experience of real pain for the first time in my life. I wanted above all for it to stop, but could only achieve this by calling a halt to the expedition.

Our sledges and equipment began to break up. We lost ski sticks and spent days man-hauling with only one and, later, with no sticks. At length, we reached the crevasses above the 9,000-foot descent of the Beardmore glacier. The daily wind chill was averaging minus 90°C. Mike again became hypothermic. His fingers, all bloody and raw, looked revolting.

Crossing the 1,000-mile polar plateau, we had seen not a single natural feature and shared the compass work but, as we began our descent to the Pacific, we came to the Trans-Antarctic mountain range. I had long planned a complex route to descend the Beardmore glacier suggested by a glaciologist and taken partly from aerial photos. As navigator, I decided to take over all navigation work during the descent. Mike was not entirely happy with this, but I had total confidence in my navigating abilities and none in anybody else's.

On many a previous journey I had learned the perils of allowing too much democracy to creep into the process of navigating. It leads too often to argument, frustration and self-doubts in the navigator. I wanted no such

Using a penknife saw-blade to make a ski-stick out of our spare ski.

pressures on my instinctive navigational processes during this most hazardous stage of the continental crossing. I preferred to risk Mike's displeasure to any relaxing of my principles of expedition leadership. I like to take democratic decision-making to the brink, but no further. Mike was very understanding, but I knew he would rightly complain the instant he felt my navigating was taking us into avoidable hazards.

The great mountaineer Reinhold Messner, despite his unrivalled experience in glacier ice-falls, had soon become hopelessly lost on the same route down the Beardmore. We had no crampons for the descent of this complex ice route, but Mike managed to use home-made rope crampons to some effect. This was just as well since he had a twisted ankle which was swollen and painful.

Of the upper stretches of the Beardmore, Shackleton wrote, 'Without crampons each step was an essay in uncertainty where many times a slip meant certain death.' The Mill glacier, which we had to cross at its conflu-

**Antarctic
mountains with
crevasse field at
ridge bottom.**

'One never notices what has been done,
one can only see what remains to be done'

MARIE CURIE

8
LEARNING
FROM FAILURE

O
n our return from Antarctica Mike and I were invited to 10 Downing Street and, later, awarded OBEs. But, five months later, a tabloid reporter produced a full-page article (based, so he claimed, on a book by Mike) which began: 'The smiles and mutual backslapping that marked the return of Fiennes and Stroud from their record-breaking Antarctic expedition was a sham, and their 95-day trek was peppered with arguments.'

Mike phoned me that evening to explain that he was furious with the journalist, who had completely misquoted him. He wrote at once to the editor to say, 'I have been bitterly hurt by the allegations that the smiles and handshakes on our return were a sham. It is not true . . . worse, it is unadulterated rubbish. I feel so bad about what was printed, I had to apologise. Despite difficulties and immense hardships, we came back smiling and acting like friends, because that is what we are. There were some arguments on the expedition, but that is hardly surprising when you have just one man's company for so long. They were not frequent, they were not bitter and they did not spoil our relationship. We have since hinted at another expedition together, and personally, I hope we are able to do so.'

Mike and I have continued to work on expeditions together to the

RF in February 2000 at Ward Hunt Island. Temperature: minus 49°C; 24-hour darkness.

present day, but both of us are still dogged by questions such as: 'Did you ever speak again to that man you did Antarctica with?' That is the power of the press. It can make an impression remain in the minds of the readers or viewers for decades after a single article or report, no matter how little truth is involved in the first place.

Our next expedition would probably have been back in the Arctic but, sadly, the world of expedition-leading is subject to many of the same pressures as any other business and one of these is the ongoing need to evolve.

To continue with my policy of attacking only those challenges as yet achieved by nobody, I was running out of polar journeys. This was not a problem faced by the world's top mountaineers because many hundreds of giant peaks and huge vertical faces still remain virgin. But there were only two Poles and this number was not going to increase.

For a year after the physical deprivations of Antarctica I wrote books and recovered bodily but, in 1995, I heard from Morag and Laurence Howell in Aberdeen that the gossip grapevine in Norway was buzzing again. Not Erling Kagge this time, but a colleague of his named Borge Ousland was planning an attempt to cross Antarctica solo and unsupported in the 1996–97 travel season. Ousland's rationale was clear. All the great polar challenges, north and south, had already been achieved by groups of two or more. All that was left was for an individual to try unaided.

Solo travel had never appealed to me. Half the fun of an expedition is the planning of it and, as with old soldiers, the shared memories afterwards. Also, since I make a living through books and talks about the expeditions, I need good photographs and film, which are difficult to get when by myself. On the plus side, however, a lone traveller can experience fewer frustrations caused by rivalry, discontent and, as with Mike and me, differences of pace.

Testing new equipment during Alpine trials.

The Howells warned me that Borge Ousland was an even better skier than Erling Kagge. This was the equivalent of a footballer even more skilled than Pele. Proof of this was not long in coming when, in the spring of 1996, Ousland reached the South Pole unsupported in a staggeringly quick forty-four days. Mike and I had taken sixty-eight days to reach the Pole during our 1993 crossing.

If I was to stay in the polar race I had eleven months in which to train hard, for Ousland would start his solo crossing attempt in October 1996. At thirty-four years of age he was at the peak of his ability. At fifty-two I was getting rusty round the edges, but Mike Stroud had the answer – the Eco Challenge Race.

'It lasts for seven days and nights,' he told me, 'and I am entering a team. You need to be super-fit to stand any chance of even finishing the three-hundred-mile course. Join my team.'

There were five of us racing against seventy-two other five-person teams from thirty-eight countries. The race took place in a remote district of the Canadian Rockies and, although we did our damnedest, we were eliminated after five days, when we slipped behind the stringent time-zones ruling. Only fourteen teams completed the course.

Mike's arduous training programme succeeded in putting me back on the road to fitness, but a month before my departure the Howells came up with alarming news. Ousland's forty-four-day polar triumph the year before had not after all been due to superhuman man-hauling strength. He had used a new-fangled, hi-tech wind-chute.

Morag, who was to join me in Antarctica to set up a radio base in the interior, was convinced that kites were the key to polar success. 'You must get one at once,' she advised.

I obtained a suitable kite from the makers in South Wales and the graphics designer of my expedition sponsor, Dyson, tried to teach me how to use it outside the Dyson factory. The lesson ended when my instructor was tugged off his feet by a gust and, airborne, let go of the control handles. The kite flew over a tree and some power-lines to land in a road, where it was run over by a Volvo. I never completed my kite training, which was a basic error. I spent eleven months becoming what one newspaper described as 'the fittest 52-year-old in Britain', but only two days mastering the complex art of kiting.

Modifying tent and gear in a hotel room in Chile prior to flying to Antarctica.

We flew to Punta Arenas in Chile and for two weeks were kept waiting there by blizzards that raged at Patriot Hills, the only commercial airstrip in Antarctica. While there I met my three rivals, all going for the same goal.

Ousland was tall and well-built with a stern and guarded manner. I was

impressed by his professionalism and focused dedication, as well as by his youth and obvious physical power. I sensed our competitive status made him reserved and that, in other circumstances, he would be friendly enough.

Another contestant was Marek Kaminski, thirty-three, a Pole from Gdansk, who the previous year had travelled by ski to both North and South Poles, the first person ever to do so in a single year. He was even bigger than Ousland, a friendly giant with whom both Morag and I quickly clicked.

The third protagonist was a powerfully built South Korean, Ho Young Heo. In fact there were six small but stocky Hos, each looking similar to the other and each with an identical sledge and equipment containers. All were extremely friendly and all professed to be going 'solo' but as a group – the soHos. They looked in many ways even more impressive than the giants Kaminski and Ousland.

When a Chilean film director asked Ousland what he 'thought of Fiennes's chances', the Norwegian replied, 'Fiennes's competitors are much, much stronger.'

A British team arrived in Punta also bound for Antarctica and one member, Clive Johnson, showed me an impressive wind-assistance device called a para-wing. This was far easier to use than my kite and, Johnson discovered, was the same model that Ousland and Kaminski had used so successfully the previous year. Trials, on a field by the main Punta graveyard, soon proved the para-wing to be infinitely superior to the kite. I immediately tried to obtain one, but the weather at Patriot Hills improved and we flew on to Antarctica the next day.

Our four expeditions were all dropped off at various well-separated spots on the Atlantic coast of the continent, and all set out within a few hours of each other.

I said a quick farewell to Morag and the crew of the ski-plane, set my compass for 165°, which was due south, and hauled hard at my 495lb load, supplies for 110 days. The race had begun.

Race? What race? The protagonists would raise their eyebrows to a journalist and protest that merely to complete a crossing attempt was enough in itself, and that coming first, while icing on the cake, was irrelevant. This, of course, is rubbish: folk without inherent competitive urges just do not involve themselves in such activities. The denial is merely advance protection against the possibility of not being first. And since a twisted ankle, a single hidden crevasse or snapped ski binding could at any time ruin any one of our endeavours, such denials are a natural part of the game plan.

During the night of 16 November, strong winds attacked my tent and

The Antarctic crossing attempt, 1996.

loosened a flap of the fly-sheet. I eased outside and was instantly plastered with wet snow. The power of the wind took my breath away and I fell backwards over my sledge, invisible under a drift. I jammed skis into the two main fly-sheet tags and pushed them three feet down into the snow. Back in the tent I felt a great desire for a chocolate bar but desisted. Every item of food must only be eaten at an exact appointed time if the rations were to last for 110 days.

I slept well through the din of the storm. The ski sticks, on which my radio antennae were strung, were blown over and in the morning I spent an hour carefully retrieving the thin antennae wire from drifts. Twice I was blown flat on my face. Clearly, if I took the tent down, I was unlikely to be able to pitch it again in such conditions. The four light alloy tent poles break easily and there were no spares. Why not? My 495lb load could quickly rise to a still less manageable total if I were to take spare parts for this, that and the other. Everything could be considered vital, but you have to draw the line somewhere. I had no comb and no reading matter bar a miniature New Testament. One pair of spare socks and underwear for one hundred days. A single-liner sleeping bag and thin-layer Karrimat. Spares were out of the question.

The temptation was to sleep out the storm and carry on only when the wind dropped below 50 knots. The white-out was no problem as there were no crevasses on the island except along its flanks, and Dyson had invented a chest-mounted gimbal-compass which allowed me to progress in the right direction even in total white-outs with everything in the world invisible except my ski-tips.

Expeditions, I reflected, were definitely changing. Morag was able to call her husband Laurence daily on her Inmarsat equipment, by fax and phone, from her tent at Patriot Hills. He was able to search websites for the latest positions of Ousland and, sometimes, Kaminski. When I next made radio contact, Morag passed this information back to me.

My skis gripped the snow and never slid backwards despite the enormous drag of the sledge because, over the past two years, new skins had been developed and new glues to keep them firmly attached to the skis. In 1993 Mike and I had wasted much time with cold fingers trying to tighten up ever-flapping skins.

I marvelled at it all, but remained aware of other things which had not changed: the weeping cold sores, the blisters developing on my feet, the crotch rot, the piles, the poisoned windburn and the lethal sunlight pouring through Antarctica's ozone hole.

Oblivious, however, to the little chip of calcium lurking unsuspected in my kidneys.

Four days from the coast the blizzard calmed and I decided to try out my kite. The idea was to hold its control lines with both hands and ski along harnessed to my heavy sledge.

Several times gusts slammed the sledge into the back of my legs and I collapsed in a welter of skis, sticks and tangled ropes. One high-speed crash gave me a painful ankle and smashed ski-tip – I bandaged both with industrial tape.

This was the learning process. Necessity is the mother of invention and for the first time I began to develop the kiting knack. To my enormous delight, I learned to catch the wind and hold it, but only in the direction which the wind dictated.

A GPS check showed that all my wonderful sailing had taken me well to the east of my intended destination and perilously close to crevasse fields. So I was forced to return to the grind of man-hauling: the difference between Formula 1 racing and carthorse riding. Everything in my tent was wet that night. Both lips wept pus from burns like cold sores, which cracked and bled when I ate chocolate.

On 18 November I made weak contact with Morag. She told me that over two days I had gained nearly thirty miles to Ousland's twenty-one miles. The following day, however, saw the arrival of a steady east wind enabling Ousland to use his para-wing and cover a staggering ninety-nine miles in two days. His skill enabled him to use winds from the west and east to propel him southwards. If only I could do likewise. I swore at my folly for not discovering para-wings before it was too late to obtain one.

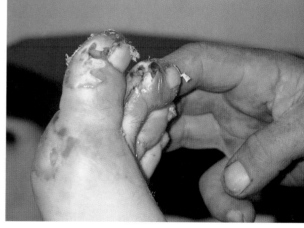

RF's foot in Antarctica.

Throughout 21–22 November there was no wind, only white-out, and both Ousland and I man-hauled due south. He managed 19 miles: I completed 19.3, despite my extra 100lb load. Not exactly catching him up, but a good sign for the 500-mile plateau ahead, where man-hauling should come into its own due to the head winds that prevailed there.

My heels developed blisters, so I strapped on foam snippets cut from my bed-mat and tried to ignore them. My chin, windburnt, became poisoned and swollen, so I lanced it with a scalpel until the swelling subsided. My eyes lost their long-distance focus after a week staring at the glare through goggles. As usual, the lids puffed up with liquid. My eyes became mere slits. I resembled a rabbit with advanced myxomatosis.

Every evening I attended to my developing crotch rot with Canestan powder and applied lengths of industrial sticky tape to raw areas. My back and hips were sore, but not as painful as on previous journeys because my harness designers had developed an effective new padding system. For the first time, life was truly bearable, almost enjoyable, on a heavy polar man-haul journey.

The sun provided no relief. It burst through the white-out one day and I was immediately too hot. I continued stripped to my underwear. Any bare strip of skin quickly burned purple because the ozone hole was at its worst at that time of year. I fashioned a head cover from a ration bag, which covered my neck and shoulders like the flap of a képi. A day later, the white-out returned, but I still managed eleven hours of non-stop man-hauling. I was well ahead of schedule.

A rare north wind and conditions of good visibility allowed me to try my luck at kiting again. Without stopping for chocolate and taking quick gulps of energy orange from my vacuum flask, I kited 117 miles in one day. I now thought I was almost certain to succeed in the entire crossing.

Before leaving Punta Arenas, Kaminski had shown me photographs of the mountains with an arrow marking the whereabouts of Frost Spur. I had a mental picture of this spur as a hard climb, but, when about six hours away from the escarpment – the best known ascent route to the plateau – three days of poor visibility ended and brilliant sunshine revealed Frost Spur dead ahead, I came to an abrupt halt, overcome by disbelief and apprehension. Then I remembered a chance remark by Ousland about Erling Kagge, who had man-hauled to the South Pole in 1993: 'I can't understand how Kagge took his gear up the spur without crampons.'

I had no crampons, only two two-inch spikes that fitted under the centre of my ski-boots. My ice axe had fallen off my sledge during the wild kite-ride, leaving me with only a twelve-inch screw-hammer. Ahead rose the spur; a crevassed and seemingly impassable barrier, an ice-sheathed wall rising to an abrupt horizon of blue sky.

I am no climber and would not have relished the ascent with a light rucksack on my back, let alone a sledge-load still weighing about 470lb. Black clouds along the eastern horizon promised further bad weather. I began to haul myself up the icy incline, but repeatedly slid backwards. Exhausted, I pitched the tent and decided to split my sledge-load into four. If I could make my first ascent while sunlight still bathed the wall of the spur, showing me the best route, I could then descend again, eat and sleep, and complete three more climbs the next day.

Only fifty feet up my hands were already cold, and the ice wall was about to switch from brilliant sunlight to deep shadow, when I was seized by vertigo. Shaking my head to break its mesmeric spell, I gingerly retrieved my ice hammer from its sledge bag and started to pick my way up the frozen face of the spur. It was four hours before I reached the top and cached my first load. Here, in a wide expanse of nothingness, I stacked the rations and marked the pile of bags with a single ski.

The journey back down to the tent took just forty minutes and, with relief, I cooked my rehydrated spaghetti bolognese and drank two pints of tea. Ten minutes after I had fallen asleep a series of katabatic wind blasts struck the tent. This went on for an hour before I realised I must move or the tent would be damaged. In a quarter of a century of travel, I had never encountered winds of such ferocious aggression.

Sleep was out of the question during the brief lulls between each fresh blast. I dismantled the tent in seconds and lashed all my gear to a fixed ice screw. I climbed the spur again, though several times the winds blew me from my fragile holds. Once I slipped thirty feet or more, desperately trying to dig the hammer's pick into the face. Gulping air, I rested shivering against the ice with the sledge dangling below me until I could resume my snail-like ascent.

The third ascent was the worst, because I took a wrong route in the poor visibility, heading too far east. That meant I had to climb twice as high to reach the rock-lined upper rim of the spur. With the clouds to the east now obscuring the escarpment, I immediately made a fourth ascent, but was too tired to manage two 25lb ration bags. So I had to descend a fifth time to retrieve them.

The final climb, with the 50lb load over my shoulders and no sledge, was easier. However, the storm clouds from the east reached the top of the spur before I did. Light snow began to fall and I could find no trace of my equipment cache or my previous tracks. I grew cold as the sweat of the climb froze on my skin. I knew that the twenty days of bagged rations over my shoulders would do me little good if I failed to find the cache.

I prayed hard and an hour later I stumbled on the dump. Such moments of relief almost make these journeys worthwhile. Hearing the news of winning a lottery jackpot could not even approach the sheer happiness of that instant when I found my cache above Frost Spur.

I could not actually see the Antarctic plateau – in fact, I could see no feature at all in any direction – but I knew I had reached the gateway to the Pole. The dangers of the ice shelf and the escarpment were behind me. For the next seventy miles there would be crevasses and wicked moraines, masses of ice debris that formed difficult barriers, but after that there was nothing but the vast open plain of the polar plateau. I ate a piece of chocolate and thought again of Borge's comment: 'Fiennes's competitors are much, much stronger.' I might yet prove him wrong. I had caught up more than seventy of the miles he had gained by sailing the east winds. Both Kaminski, the Pole, and the tough little Korean man-haulers were well over 100 miles behind me after only seventeen days of travel.

I felt elated. To hell with being too old. It's all in the mind. At this stage of our 1993 Antarctic crossing, Mike Stroud and I had already been in a state of semi-starvation and severe physical decline. Yet this time I was still feeling on top form, no more hungry than after a day's training on Exmoor. I was accustomed to the raw skin, poisoned blisters and screaming ligaments, which returned on every man-haul trip.

The pain in my ankle from the sailing crash was better now, as were my heels. Life was good and my competitive urge bubbled up as I set out the next morning, the sledge dragging through the soft new snow.

If only the east winds stay absent all the way to the Pole, I thought, I will beat Ousland. The harder the man-hauling, the quicker I will catch him. Then, on the far side of the Pole, the winds will be behind both of us and my new-found kite skills will cope with his para-wing expertise. After all, in a single day on Berkner Island, my 117 miles were greater even than Ousland's best day's sail to date. Such were my thoughts.

Only twelve hours later I made radio contact with Morag and my optimism was dashed. Ousland had used his wonderful skill at para-wing control of flank-winds to travel 134 miles in only four days. Ahead of me stretched the Jaberg glacier and the heavily crevassed snow-fields. This was one of the most wild and beautiful places in Antarctica and, in parts, one of the most dangerous.

On 2 December, Morag told me through whining static that our charity, Breakthrough, had already raised over £1 million towards the £3 million needed to fund a London breast cancer research centre. The further I progressed, the more money we would raise. This impetus had always proved an enormous mental help at times when the going was especially hard and the temptation to give up at its strongest.

The new snow continued to grip my sledge runners, making every step a battle. For long periods my skis disappeared and often snagged one another, tripping me up. My speed dropped to a mile an hour, sometimes even less. The leather upper halves of my ski boots came away from the plastic foot shells and needed four hours of re-stitching.

On the twentieth day of my journey, I was already ten days ahead of my previous crossing. Not because of faster man-hauling, but entirely due to the single day of southerly kiting.

When the sun was out, sweat poured down my face. My forehead and the back of my neck were seared. The ultraviolet light pouring through the ozone hole was far more noticeable than on my journey with Mike Stroud in 1993.

For seven years of man-haul journeys, Mike and I had developed a practice of never indulging in rest days en route. Even Norway's top man-haulers made a habit of resting for one day in twenty, but Mike, a nutritionist and doctor, agreed with me that the chances of success were greater without rest days, so long as you learned to control your mind.

Panic arises from fear of failure, leading to the sudden collapse of the reservoir of willpower needed to sustain enormous effort and discomfort for long periods. The best way to keep panic at bay is to have prepared a store of 'positive thoughts' to produce on demand.

Imminent danger, such as an approaching crevasse field, is a great help, since you can fill your mind with thoughts about what to do if you plunge into the maw of a 100-foot fissure. Such thoughts can be stretched out to help the long hours and slow miles pass by without constantly dwelling on the sheer size of the task ahead and the slow and painful breakdown of your body. Mike's term for getting lost in his thoughts was 'mind-travelling'.

Sometimes I would check my watch and find to my disgust that a really excellent run of absorbing thoughts had actually eliminated only a few minutes of reality. I often wished to howl like a dog, anything to master my thoughts and banish the insistent desire to halt because the whole task was simply too hard and hurt too much.

I would imagine that my grandfather, a pioneer in Canada and Africa, my father and my uncle, both killed in the world wars, and my living family were all right behind me, willing me on.

As the last mountain peaks passed by with infinite slowness, I imagined that I was hauling a heavy sledge at a gulag in Siberia, that I was undernourished and poorly clothed, that I would be doing this every day for many years and that the only alternative was death. My chant, in time to the creak of my sticks, was 'Gulag, gulag, gulag'.

Two minor niggles chased me. I had seldom travelled alone before,

except on SAS selection courses in the Brecon Beacons long ago. I believe solo journeys in remote places are irresponsible. Anybody can fall into a crevasse. In the smaller fissures, you can get jammed in a smooth ice bottle-neck as the crevasse narrows. The warmth of your body will cause you to slide downwards and wedge you irretrievably until you die. With a second person carrying safety ropes, there is a chance of rescue.

Hypothermia can strike any polar traveller. It happened to Mike only two days short of reaching the South Pole. Had he been alone, he would certainly have died. Quite a reasonable way to go, if you think about it, but another reason I believe solo trips to be irresponsible.

On the night of my twenty-third day, Morag sent me a message from Ousland's base leader at Patriot Hills. Ousland had passed the moraine zone in conditions of good visibility and had kindly radioed to warn me of an uncharted crevasse field. By the time I received the information, I had already passed the danger, but I was grateful for his thoughtfulness.

For the first time in two weeks my crotch and thighs were pain-free. The blisters and ulcers on both feet were healing and the sun blisters on my lips had dispersed.

On my twenty-fifth day, I was sick a few minutes after breakfast gruel. I felt faint and started out four hours behind schedule on a fine sunny day, neither too hot nor too cold. In six hours I man-hauled six miles despite a long, steep climb. The improved surface continued, but I felt queasy and took two Imodium tablets.

Behind me the deep tracks of my runners disappeared to the north, where countless mountain peaks shimmered as though floating on waves of air. Ahead lay only a blue sky and the gently sloping snow-fields leading without further obstruction to the South Pole. I was halfway to the pole and 125 miles ahead of the point Mike and I had reached in the same time in 1993. I tried not to feel over-optimistic. Things could still go wrong.

To my surprise, I was violently sick again after eating my evening meal, a delicious mixture of ghee milk fat with rehydrated shepherd's pie and Smash. I stared at the results on the tent floor and wondered how I could recycle the mess, since I had towed that ration for 400 miles and it represented energy for ten miles of further man-hauling.

I informed Morag that night that I had been sick, but was uncertain why, since I did not have diarrhoea. She told me to call her at any time if the symptoms persisted so she could relay advice from the camp doctor.

Two hours later the first cramps attacked my gut and I recognised at once the symptoms of a kidney stone blockage. I lit my cooker and heated water.

I would flush the bloody thing out of my system. Drown it with water. The pains were impressive. Groaning and talking aloud, I wrenched open the medical pack that Mike had meticulously prepared in the knowledge of my previous kidney stone attack in 1990. On that occasion we had been stationary at a Soviet science station on a remote ice floe so Mike had borrowed drugs from a Russian medic.

I gulped down morphine substitute tablets, two Buscopan anti-pain pills and inserted a Voltarol suppository for quick pain relief. Within half an hour the initial pains, which I think I can safely describe as excruciating, had dulled to a background throb. But the relief did not last.

For six hours, every hour on the hour, I tried to call Morag. However, atmospheric disturbances prevented any communication until the next morning. The weather was excellent. I yearned to be on my way. Since I was eating nothing and using fuel only to heat snow for water, rather than to heat the tent, I was not technically reducing my overall chances of success, but Ousland was ahead of me and widening the distance. Kaminski and the Koreans were creeping up from behind. But there was no way I could carry on until I had shifted the stone from my urinary tract.

When I finally made brief contact with Morag, the lady doctor at her camp – a former flying medic from north-west Australia – advised me to take painkillers every six hours and drink lots of water.

For twenty-four hours, possibly the least enjoyable period I can remember ever having spent, I writhed about in the tent. I took more painkillers than the doctor had advised and drank a great deal of water, but the stone failed to shift and the pains from my lower stomach, back and sides stayed with me.

At 11am on 27 December, I decided that the danger of irreparable damage to my kidneys, as well as the risk of running out of painkillers, was too great a price to pay for the chance of being first to cross Antarctica solo. I pulled the pin of my emergency beacon which, a few hours later, informed a satellite signal watcher in England, who called Morag, who in turn alerted the Twin Otter ski-plane crew at Patriot Hills as to my exact position.

Nine hours later, with the fine weather beginning to change, the Twin Otter landed by my tent. Throughout the flight back to Patriot Hills, the Australian doctor fed morphine into my blood system through a drip. I was soon completely stoned and in wonderful, painless bliss.

Morag called my medical insurers, who advised immediate evacuation to a clinic in Punta Arenas. The weather, miraculously, held just long enough for me to fly on a scheduled Hercules flight to Punta. After an exhaustive

**Amphibious trials
in the Bering
Straits, Alaska,
1998.
L to R: Steve
Signal, Charles
Whitaker and
Granville Baylis.**

series of X-rays, an enema, and fluid injections, the surgeon sent a report to my insurers, who advised that should I return to Antarctica, as I hoped, they could no longer cover any further stone-related costs. Although the stone had shifted once the morphine had relaxed my nervous system, the condition could return at any time. Any future evacuation flight would cost over £100,000. With enormous reluctance, I accepted the end of the expedition.

Ousland went on to cross Antarctica in an amazing fifty-five days, managing to sail for well over three-quarters of the entire distance, avoiding the drudge and the toil of man-hauling. On his arrival at Scott Base my signal was the first to congratulate him. Kaminski and the soHos reached the Pole too late to continue onwards.

Using wind assistance with kites or para-wings that can use winds from 180° is very different from the use of following-wind devices, such as the parachutes or dinghy sails used by Amundsen, Shackleton, Scott and, in 1993, by Mike Stroud and me with singular lack of success.

Had my kidneys behaved themselves, I am sure Ousland would still have beaten me across Antarctica, and I would have maintained my lead on the others. My big mistake was to concentrate on man-haul fitness rather than becoming a wind-assistance expert like Ousland. Businesses that do not move with the times get left behind.

Dyson raised £1.7 million through the expedition and helped set up Europe's first dedicated breast cancer research centre. If I had completed the journey, the sum raised would have been a good deal more.

For the next two years, while writing books and helping Ginnie with the cattle on Exmoor, I planned a Land Rover journey to drive around the world's landmass, from the most west-erly point in the Republic of Ireland 23,000 miles through Europe, Russia and Canada to the eastern tip of Newfoundland. We spent a good deal of time modifying our vehicles so that they could 'swim' in up to force seven ocean conditions and, also, climb mountain sides in deep snowdrifts. We rehearsed in iceberg-strewn waters in the Bering Straits and successfully crossed the high mountains between the Alaskan west coast and the village of Nome. Everything was ready for a successful venture.

Charles Whitaker and Granville Baylis during Land Rover trials in Alaska.

I shared the planning with Canadian and Russian co-leaders and all went well until BMW bought Land Rover and removed our entire budget overnight. Such is life.

Early in 1999 I began training for an Arctic journey and was paid a handsome publisher's advance for a book about it. The idea was simple: an attempt to reach the North Pole solo and unsupported by the direct route from the Arctic coastline of North America, one of the few polar challenges still to be achieved.

Mike Stroud helped organise the vital calorific planning in conjunction with Brian Welsby, the nutritionist I had worked with for sixteen years.

I arrived at Resolute Bay in northern Canada on 5 February 2000, not long after the sun had reappeared there for the first time in five months. I was met there by Morag Howell who had become the base manager at Resolute Bay for First Air, the airline which would fly me north to the Arctic Ocean start-line.

There are two modes of unsupported north polar man-hauling: very fast or very slow. The Norwegians are the chief proponents of the 'Speedy Gonzales' approach: light equipment, medium-range calorific intake, superb fitness and, above all, the brilliant skiing technique that comes from cross-country ski-racing since childhood.

At fifty-five I could not hope to reach the Pole in less than fifty days, the period that Norwegian skiers were aiming for. I would have to go for the tortoise approach, which I estimated would take eighty-five days. For safety I would carry ninety days' food. This alone would weigh more than 230lb, with fuel to melt ice to rehydrate it coming to another 60lb. All additional gear – tent, sleeping bag, mat, cooking kit, rope, axe, shovel, grapnel hook, spare ski, spare clothes, repair kit, medical kit, camera, shotgun, lithium batteries, fluorescent marker poles, paddle – would total another 220lb; too much for a single sledge travelling in Arctic rubble ice, so I had to use two sledges.

Altogether, I would need to haul 510lb and relay two loads, which meant every mile gained to the north would involve three travelled on the ground.

Night trials in Alaska with amphibious Land Rovers.

**Opposite:
RF conducting amphibious sledge trials on the Thames, January 2000.**

**Overleaf:
RF towing 495lb prototype Arctic sledge, January 2000.**

This added to the dangers of a one-sledge trip, in that blizzards and white-outs are common. In such conditions perspective is wiped out and ski tracks become invisible. You are in a world of cotton wool, or white night, able to see only your own body: all else is a grey-white blur. You may fall into the water or crash into a thirty-foot-high wall with no visual warning. To all intents you are blind.

In such conditions the need to relay sledges involves a potentially lethal risk – once you have parked the first sledge and set off for your second load, you may never find it. At some point you will decide, because of the cold, to return to the first sledge. But it too may be impossible to find. You will then die.

I had no option but to take two sledges, so my schedule took the extra mileage into account. If I could travel north for ten hours every day for eighty days, with no rest day for injuries, bad weather or watery obstacles, my best progress would be 500 yards a day for the first three days, 1.4 miles daily for the next thirty days, 4.5 miles daily until day 58 and then, with a single sledge only, 11 miles daily to the Pole.

Many unsupported treks to the Pole have been scuppered by stretches of open water blocking the way north without temperatures low enough to refreeze the sea water. To avoid such delays I had two buoyancy tubes that fastened to either side of my bigger sledge making it buoyant even when fully laden and with me sitting atop its load wielding a paddle.

Conferring in base hut prior to the start with 'Mac' Mackenney.

On 14 February we flew to the most northerly of Canada's meteorological stations, at Eureka, where musk oxen and wolves roam the hills around the airstrip. After refuelling, my friend from many earlier journeys, Karl Z'berg, piloted the Twin Otter 100 miles further north to the edge of the Arctic Ocean and the conical hill at the north end of Ward Hunt Island, the starting point of most North Pole attempts. With lurching bumps, we were down. As the door opened, I felt the bitter cold of 84° North in winter. The sun would not show its face here for three more weeks, and then only for thirty minutes a day.

Meanwhile, I would travel by moonlight and head torch powered by

Opposite: Further preparation for the 2000 expedition.

lithium batteries. Once the ski-plane had gone, I took a bearing to geographical north. The compass needle pointed to magnetic north 300 miles west of Resolute Bay and 600 miles south of my position. I had to set a magnetic lay-off of 98°, then wait a minute for the needle to settle in the less than normal viscosity of its alcohol-filled housing. I could not use the North Star as a marker because it was almost directly overhead. Nor, pulling a sledge, could I use my GPS position-finder for direction.

The clothing policy I had evolved over twenty-eight years of polar expeditions was based on non-stop movement and light, breathable clothes. Any halt, however brief, could lead to hypothermia. Once my metabolism was up and running, pumping blood furiously to my extremities, I took off my duck-down duvet and stuffed it in the sledge next to my vacuum flask and twelve-bore pump shotgun. Now I was wearing only a thin wickaway vest and longjohns under a black jacket and trousers made of 100 per cent Ventile cotton. Cotton is not windproof so body heat is not sealed in. Alas, no modern clothing, such as Gore-tex, is completely breathable so, when pulling excessive loads over difficult terrain, the man-hauler perspires. The sweat turns to ice inside the clothing and can quickly lead to hypothermia. Cotton is still the best compromise, provided you keep your blood running fast, except when in your tent and sleeping bag.

My schedule allowed two days to descend the soft snow-fields of Ward Island's ice shelf to the edge of the sea. But I kept going without a rest and established both sledges at the coastline within seven hours. This boded well, for the sledges were running easily despite their full loads, the low temperature and soft, deep snow. Geoff Somers, an experienced polar guide, had advised me to include a cantilever design in the sledge moulds. The sledge-makers Snowsled had done so, and the result was excellent.

After seven hours of hard man-hauling, I was cold and tired. I erected the tent in six minutes and started the cooker in four. These two acts, which I had practised thousands of times, are the key to survival, and with two usable hands can be performed easily in extreme temperatures, high winds and blizzards. I got into my sleeping bag, drank some energy drink, ate chocolate and set my alarm watch for three hours. The weather was clear when I woke and the sea ice quiet to the north, a sign that the ice floes were not on the move.

The Moon had vanished behind the hills, meaning I would not be able to differentiate clearly between solid ice and thinly skinned zones, so the overall ice-silence indicating static floes was a bonus. I re-stowed the big sledge, moving rapidly to keep my body core temperature up. I decided to take the smaller sledge first. Its load was 210lb, a third less than the eight-foot sledge. The ice floes that are blown south against this northern coastline of the Canadian archipelago shatter against the ice shelf and blocks up to twenty-five feet high tumble over one another, often forming huge ramparts that run east–west for miles. Behind them a scene of utter chaos can meet the despairing man-hauler, slab upon slab of fractured ice block as far as the weary eye can see.

Over the past fifteen years with Mike Stroud, I had three times broken the current world record for unsupported travel to the North Pole. Each time the ice conditions north of Ward Hunt Island were invariably bad to horrible. I saw that this year the walls and rubble were split everywhere by recent breakage. New ice floes of twilight grey zigzagged through the obstacles wherever I looked. My schedule of only 500 yards a day for the first three miles from the start began to look optimistic.

I pressed on over the fissure dividing land from sea and into a broad belt of rubble. I took my skis off. For a few hundred yards I would have to haul each sledge over a vista similar to that of post-war Berlin. Between each ice slab soft, deep snow covered the fissures. I often fell into traps, sinking waist deep.

I came to a wall of slabs fifteen feet high and decided to test the simple pulley system devised by my base leader, 'Mac' Mackenney. I attached it to the big sledge, which I had hauled first to the wall, and tugged it jerkily up the 45° slope. With the 300lb sledge at the top of the wall, I detached the tiny grapnel hook and rolled up the pulley line. Too late I heard movement, and leapt towards the sledge which quickly gathered momentum in its slide over the edge of the wall. I managed to grab the rear end, but my 200lb body weight was not enough. The far side of the wall was a sheer fifteen-foot drop on to sharp ice blocks. I landed hard and was winded but unhurt.

At first the sledge looked undamaged, but closer inspection revealed a sixteen-inch tear under the bow, presumably where the sharp edge of an ice block had made contact with the 300lb falling hull. I tried handling the sledge, but snow was caught in the damaged section and dragging it became difficult. Also, the floatability of the sledge's hull, designed to be completely watertight, was compromised.

There was no alternative but to head back to the hut on Ward Hunt Island and find substitute materials to effect a repair.

In the mid-1980s we had erected a canvas cover over the steel skeleton of a hut long abandoned by scientists and installed a couple of wind-powered generators to provide electricity. With minimal safety gear in a bag, I skied for two hours back up my own outward trail and then, via the Twin Otter's landing strip, headed east along the base of the mountain. The old huts looked like a ghost camp, unchanged over the twelve years since my last visit. After an hour spent digging out the door of our old hut, I gained entry. There were a few tools and canvas materials, so I decided to bring the sledge back to make it watertight and capable of towing in all conditions. I skied back to the sledges and loaded minimal camping gear on to the smaller one. Then I lashed the damaged sledge on top. Uphill through soft snow was slow going, some seven hours back to the hut.

I put my tent up inside the hut. The temperature outside had fallen to minus 49°C with a bitter breeze. With the cooker on, a hot drink inside me and fully clothed, I began the repairs. Some hours later I was back at the ice edge, happy that my work had made the sledge easy to tow, even in soft snow and pretty much watertight.

I found my previous trail easily enough to the island's coastline. I camped on thin ice but woke to hear all manner of noises: cracking and rumbling, then silence. Then, a nearby and frightening roar that galvanised me into movement from the depths of my four-layer sleeping bag. The Moon was full, the scenery startlingly beautiful. Moonshadows played about the upended ice blocks and the ice shapes took on an uncanny resemblance to animals, castles or giant mushrooms.

Sledge repair at Ward Hunt Island, February 2000.

Fearful of imminent upheaval due to the tidal influence of the full Moon fracturing the floes and the notoriety of the first four miles of ice to the north of Ward Hunt, I pressed on northwards. I dared not take either sledge too far, because the surface between the rubble fields consisted of very thin ice through which my probing ski-stick passed with ease into the dark waters below. After eight hours I had moved both sledges more than a mile to the north. My morale was high for the sledges ran well whatever the surface, far better than any previous design. My mental arithmetic raced ahead and I estimated a Pole arrival in only seventy days.

I kept an eye open for a good campsite. Sea ice grows at a rate of two to three feet a year. Ice floes that survive intact for more than two years are easy to identify, for the broken blocks that litter their surfaces will be leached of salt by two or more years of summer melt. The wind and snow round them into hummocks. Such floes can be at least eight feet thick and more likely to withstand great pressure from neighbouring floes. They can provide good landing strips for ski-planes. Above all, the surface snow will provide good drinking water. Unfortunately, time passed without the appearance of any floe older than a few months. Indeed, the area began to show increasing signs of recently open and only partially refrozen water. My ski-stick sank through the surface skin frequently now, forcing me to detour to safer ice.

I had been travelling for well over the intended ten hours and was making good progress. I ate a chocolate bar every two hours to ward off hypothermia, but was beginning to tire so I decided to camp on any flat surface that looked solid. I came to a zone of interlacing fractures. The Moon had vanished, but whenever I stopped I heard the grumble of ice on the move. To avoid a trench of black water, I mounted a bridge of twelve-inch-thick slabs, buckled by floe pressure. I had the small sledge with me and the big one 500 yards to the south. I clambered over the slabs with my skis on. The sledge followed easily in my wake.

There was no warning. A slab tilted suddenly under the sledge, which responded to gravity and, unbalancing me, pulled me backwards. I fell on my back and slid down the slab. The noise that followed was the one I most hate to hear in the Arctic, a splash as the sledge fell into the sea.

I kicked out with my skis and flailed at the slab with both hands. One ski boot plunged into the sea and one gloved hand found an edge of a static slab. Taking a firm grip, I pulled my wet foot and ski out of the water and managed to unfasten my man-haul harness. I was already beginning to shiver. I squirmed around until I could sit on a flatter slab to inspect the sledge in the gloom.

It was under water, but not sinking. I hauled on the traces, but they were jammed somewhere under the slabs. Seventy days' worth of food and thirty of fuel were on that sledge – and the communications gear: without it the expedition was over. A nearby slab crashed into the sea: the ice was moving. I had to save the sledge quickly. Soon I would be dangerously cold.

With my feet (skis off) hooked around a slab, I lay on my stomach and stretched my left arm under the slab to free the sledge trace. I pushed up my sledge jacket sleeve and took off my outer mitt. In retrospect I may have been better off keeping it on, but I had to feel for the submerged rope.

For a minute or so I could not find the snag. Then, by jiggling the rope sharply, it came free. I pulled hard and the sodden sledge rose to the surface.

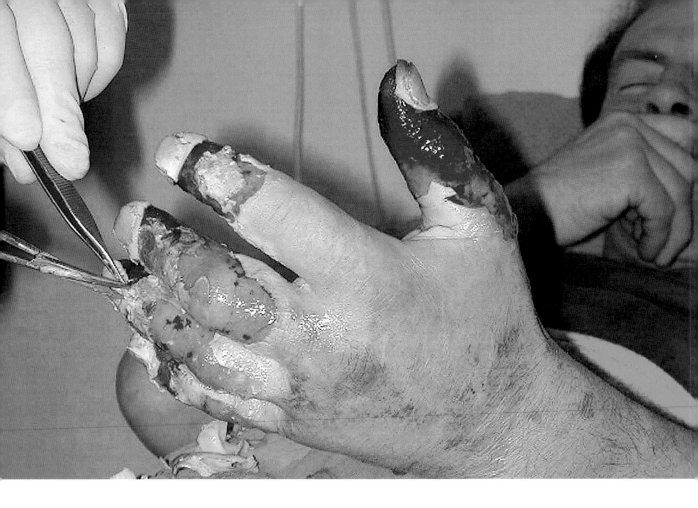

RF not liking surgical treatment at Ottawa Hospital. All five fingers were later amputated.

My wet hand was numb, but I could not replace the mitt until the sledge was out of the sea. Gradually the prow rose on to a slab and water cascaded off its canvas cover. Minutes later the sledge was on 'dry land'. I danced about like a madman. Both my mitts were back on and I used my 'cold hands revival technique' to restore life to the numb fingers. This involves a fast windmill motion with the fingers on the outside of the resulting centrifugal orbit. Usually my blood returns painfully to all my fingers: this time it did not.

I took off the mitt and felt the dead hand. The fingers were ramrod stiff and ivory white. They might as well have been wooden. I knew that if I let my good hand go even partially numb, I would be unable to erect the tent and start the cooker, which I needed to do quickly for I was shivering in my thin hauling-clothes.

I returned to the big sledge. The next thirty minutes were a nightmare. The sledge-cover zip jammed. Precious minutes went by before I could free it and unpack the tent. By the time I had eased a tent-pole into one of the four pole-sleeves my teeth were chattering violently and my good hand was numb. I had to get the cooker going in minutes or it would be too late. I crawled into the partially erect tent, closed its door-zip and began a twenty-minute battle to start the cooker. I could not use the petrol lighter with my fingers, but I found some matches I could hold in my teeth.

Starting an extremely cold petrol cooker involves careful priming so that just the right amount of fuel seeps into the pad below the fuel jet. The cold makes washers brittle and the priming plunger sticky. Using my teeth and a numb index finger, I finally worked the pump enough to squirt fuel on to the pad, but was slow in shutting the valve: when I applied the match a three-foot flame reached to the roof. Luckily I had had a custom-made flame lining installed, so the tent was undamaged. And the cooker was alight – one of the best moments of my life.

RF's frostbitten fingers three weeks after the accident.

Slowly and painfully some life came back into the fingers of my good hand. An hour later, with my body warm again, I unlaced my wet boot. Only two toes had been affected. Soon they would exhibit big blood blisters and lose their nails, but they had escaped true frostbite. All around the tent cracking noises sounded above the steady roar of the cooker. I was in no doubt as to the fate of my bad hand. I had seen enough frostbite in others to realise I was in serious trouble. I had to get to a hospital quickly to save some fingers from the surgeon's knife. I hated to leave the warmth of the tent. Both hands were excruciatingly painful. I battered ice off the smaller sledge, unloaded it and hauled it back to the big sledge. I set out in great trepidation. Twice my earlier tracks had been cut by newly open leads, but luckily both needed only small diversions to detour the open water. Five hours later I was back on the ice shelf. I erected the tent properly and spent three hours massaging my good hand and wet foot over the cooker.

I drank hot tea and ate chocolate. I felt tired and dizzy, but the wind was showing signs of rising and I knew I should not risk high wind chill. The journey to the hut took for ever. Once I fell asleep on the move and woke in a trough of soft snow well away from my intended route.

When I came to the hut I erected the tent on the floor, started the cooker and prepared the communications gear, which we call a Flobox after 'Flo' Howell. I spoke to Morag in Resolute Bay. She promised to evacuate me the following day using a Twin Otter due to exchange weathermen at Eureka.

The fingers on my left hand began to grow great liquid blisters. The pain was bad so I raided my medical stores for drugs. The next day I found an airstrip near the hut and marked its ends with kerosene rags. When I heard the approaching ski-plane, I lit the rags and an hour later I was on my way to Eureka.

Thirty-six hours after that I was at Ottawa General Hospital watching as a surgeon stripped skin and sliced blisters from my fingers. For the next two weeks I received daily treatment in a hyperbaric oxygen chamber.

Back in England I allowed the damaged tissue to slowly heal in readiness for the end-knuckles of the thumb and each finger to be amputated. I took penicillin for four months to keep gangrene out of the open cracks, where the damaged but live flesh met the dead and blackened finger-ends. By the end of June I was able to saw the dead finger-ends off with a fret-saw. This helped the new stump areas heal in readiness for final surgery by an expert plastic surgeon.

I suppose, over twenty-six years of polar travel, the frostbite odds were always narrowing. This time they caught up with me, which was a shame because everything was looking good, the gear was excellent and I felt fit for the job. There is, of course, never any point in crying over spilt milk because in order to win at some of the big ones, you will always lose at others along the way. The key is to learn from the failures and then to keep going.◆

The Lessons Learned

There is never any point crying over spilt milk because
in order to win at some of your big goals
you are bound to lose at others along the way

◆

You can only count on staying physically fit by
regular ongoing training. The older you are,
the more this unfortunate fact will apply to you

◆

It is sensible to diversify, to be ready to plough a new furrow,
for you can never count on the status quo

◆

'Only the fit survive'

ROBERT SERVICE

9

FIGHTING ANNO DOMINI

Nearly twenty years ago, *The Guinness Book of Records* nominated me for their World Hall of Fame as the 'world's greatest living explorer'. They also nominated Paul McCartney in the world of music and Billie Jean King for sports, reaching their results simply by adding up the number of world records achieved. Since one can only achieve the status of 'explorer' by actually exploring, not just breaking geographical records and achieving 'firsts', this sobriquet must have largely come my way due to our mapping journey through virgin regions of Antarctica back in the 1970s.

To stay ahead or at least abreast of my rivals in the expedition business over the past three decades has above all involved keeping physically fit, working with the best of individual team mates, and knowing about my rivals, who they are and what they are up to.

Over the years my main competition has come chiefly from Norway: Ragnar Thorsketh in the 1970s, Erling Kagge in the '80s and Borge Ousland in the '90s.

In Russia the chief polar protagonists have included Dmitry Shparo, Misha Malakov and Vladimir Chukov. In Canada Richard Weber has shone brilliantly, Messner briefly from Italy, Arved Fuchs likewise from Germany,

Training on Exmoor, 1999.

Jean-Louis Etienne from France and the late Naomi Uemura from Japan.

At home in Britain there have been a healthy number of achievers in genuine polar firsts including Vivian Fuchs, Wally Herbert, Charles Swithinbank, Robert Swan, Roger Mear, Mike Stroud, Charlie Burton and Geoff Somers.

Thanks to Laurence and Morag Howell, our group had been able to keep close tabs on all-comers so that we knew where our own priorities should concentrate.

In terms of choosing the best people for our group and then keeping them involved over many years, I have mentioned in this book the selection methods used, but luck also has a lot to do with it. Luck brings the people along and selection methods decide whether they are the best material for the project being planned. If they are happy they will stay involved. With Charlie, Ollie and Mike as my fellow travellers over a twenty-year period, I was blessed with the very best in the business.

The other ingredient vital to staying ahead, that of physical fitness, is a lot less simple. Once you know your rivals' intentions, and have your team in hand, you can count on a basic scenario. Once you are fit, however, you can only count on staying that way by constant training. You can never relax

for long and the older you are the more this holds good, especially past the magic age of forty-seven years, when the tide really begins to turn with a vengeance.

Although Charlie Burton is more or less my age, Mike Stroud is eleven years younger and not easy to keep up with. After our continental-crossing journey I received a barrage of letters enquiring about my fitness regime. I tried to respond helpfully, but anything less than a complete answer was liable to prove of minimal benefit. There are many sides to maintaining personal fitness and any advice on the subject needs to encompass every facet – exercise, food intake and mental approach – so I wrote a book entitled *Fit for Life* containing the rules which for twenty years have worked well enough to keep me in trim.

Left: RF using a climbing machine for overall strength and cardiovascular fitness.

Opposite: Towing a simulated sledge-load of tyres on Exmoor. Man-hauling muscles need specific training.

Unfortunately, the inner desire to keep going for that run or yet another visit to the gym (whatever the weather and your hectic schedule) does not get stronger with the passage of the years.

At the age of forty-nine, the UK Army Personnel Research Establishment, which for years had evaluated athletes and special forces individuals for demanding tasks, such as NASA space missions, subjected me to their tests. The supervising officer summarised my fitness as being 'in line with that of a 21-year-old athlete in peak form'.

Unfortunately, only six years later, at fifty-five, I needed a similar state of fitness for a demanding expedition, but I had just spent twelve months at a desk writing the biography of a Welsh accountant. This was my second biography. The first, entitled *The Feather Men*, had been a number-one bestseller in the UK. My rationale in taking time off to write these non-expedition books was the need to diversify. I knew I would never get another Occidental-type job and I was increasingly aware that the expeditions demanded a high standard of fitness which was inconsistent with being middle-aged. Just as pretty actresses need to think about diversifying into comedy or any genre not totally dependent on their looks, I needed to try my hand at books about other people's activities.

I needed a firm mental boost to revive my enthusiasm for a hard training schedule. I called Mike Stroud. Would he enter a team for another Eco Challenge Endurance Race? And might I join it? Sadly, Mike was too busy having taken over huge responsibilities at Southampton General Hospital, but a cardiologist friend of his, an ex-SAS man, agreed to put together a team and enter the 1998 race. We duly arrived in Morocco that summer with a team which included Hélène Diamantides, Britain's fastest female 100-kilometre endurance racer, and Steven Seaton, an accomplished marathon runner and the editor of *Runner's World* magazine.

I had trained like a dingbat under the watchful eye of a member of the British Olympic sailing squad's training team, Jonathan 'Adolf' Beevers, but the

Left: RF undergoing a fitness test in Mike Stroud's Farnborough research chamber.

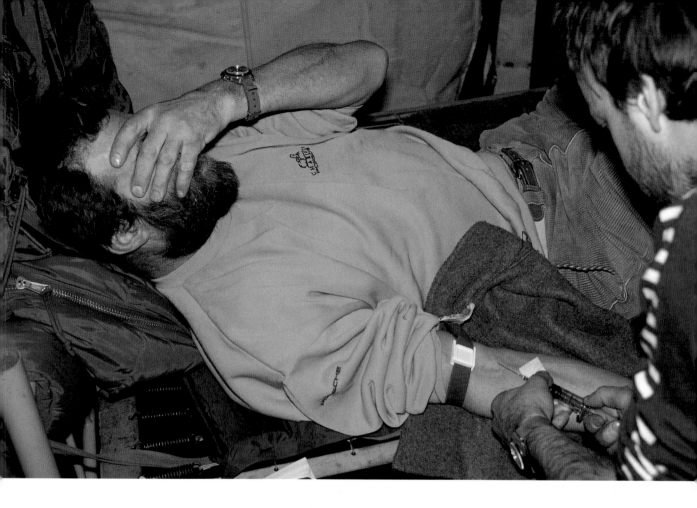

Mike's
physiological
research
programme
continued over
four of our polar
expeditions, and
was not always
pleasant.

Mountain bike

section of the

1998 Eco

Challenge Race

in Morocco.

L to R: Søren, RF

and Steven Seaton.

Moroccan course was nonetheless exhausting. After four days our team lay at twenty-ninth out of fifty-five starters, but our team leader had to drop out and Hélène, though strong as ever, saw no point in our continuing as an un-ranked team.

Because a team can only keep going in the remote regions where these races are held with a minimum of three, Steven and I joined up with the remnants of Team California. For three more days and nights all went well, but then both Americans fell out with enteritis. Luckily, a member of Team Germany broke his leg, so we joined the remaining Germans. Their captain became violently sick on the seventh night at 15,000 feet in the High Atlas and was removed by helicopter. Three of us finally completed the entire course in nine days and nights.

Anybody can enter an endurance race, but the standard has become very high with a growing number of ex-Olympic champion runners, cyclists and canoeists joining their country's team. To help my preparations for my 2000 Arctic expedition I asked Steven Seaton, who took over as team leader after Morocco, if I could stay in the team for the 2000 race. Sarah Odell, who has won the infamous Raid Gauloises in Tibet and is one of a handful of the world's top female endurance racers, joined us. Then Pete James, Britain's most successful endurance racer, joined our ranks. This influx of quality was due to a new ruling that individuals could only race for their own country. Sarah had previously raced for France and New Zealand, while Pete had come second in Morocco racing for Australia.

Right: As part of the 1999 Eco Challenge training, RF completes the London Marathon in three and a half hours.

Overleaf: With Ginnie on the farm on Exmoor.

The team set yardsticks to achieve through the months leading up to the Patagonia race. To fail at these 'trials', I realised, might endanger my place in the team. Competitors had to complete the 120-mile Devizes to Westminster canoe race in a reasonable time. Steven and I paddled non-stop for twenty-six hours to reach Big Ben, an improvement of three hours over the previous year. Another such trial was to run the London Marathon in three and a half hours. I had run my first marathon ten years before when I was only forty-five and took 4 hours 50 minutes, so I had

to train hard for five months and still only just managed it in 3 hours 30 minutes and 29 seconds.

In December 1999, racing against fifty-four of the best teams in the world, we finished fourteenth. The race was held in the Patagonian mountains, a rugged and unspoilt wilderness. I was twenty-three years older than the rest of the team and eight years older than any other competitor in the race. This boosted my confidence immediately prior to going back to the Arctic.

I would love to remain in one of the British endurance teams at least until I am sixty, and this objective gives me a wonderfully strong incentive back at home to stir my stumps, whatever the Exmoor weather, and keep training.

It became clear, as the over-fifty years went by, that the struggle to stay fit required ever more time and effort. I had been voted Pipe Smoker of the Year, but now I had to give up smoking. I had been a gluttonous chocoholic, but now I had to tone down my sweet-tooth binges and buy disgusting things like dried figs in an attempt to wean myself from such true pleasures as Maltesers. And, instead of making do with hour-long runs twice a week, I needed a minimum of three 2½-hour runs with plenty of uphill stuff en route. Worst of all, I had to start gym-work for basic upper body strength, merely to maintain muscle which, prior to my fiftieth year, had maintained itself at a reasonable level without my having to waste time with weight-training.

The plus side of all this training is the confidence which comes with knowing you can keep up with top athletes half your age. It would be all too easy to miss out on the training and start accepting that there are unavoidable limitations caused by the passage of time. Once that acceptance is in place, the inevitable next phase is vegetation and a steady physical degeneration leading to loss of confidence and a greater proneness to debilitating illnesses, cancers and heart troubles.

Any loss of confidence will have a knock-on effect on your relationships with business colleagues, friends and even close family. Dr Hammer remained supremely self-confident and a hyperactive CEO of a great global corporation into his nineties. He stressed many times that his durability was due largely to keeping fit through daily exercise.

Anybody, including tramps who have spent their lives wandering with no aim but survival, can learn by their mistakes if they bother to analyse them. This book is intended as such an analysis, setting each new venture in its context and trying, with the benefit of hindsight, to highlight the lessons learned.◆

At home with part-husky dog Pingo.

APPENDIX

The individuals involved with the expeditions described
in this book include:

Norway, 1967

Peter Loyd, Simon Gault, Nick Holder, Don Hughes,
Martin Grant-Peterkin, Vanda Allfrey

Nile, 1969

Peter Loyd, Nick Holder, Charles Westmorland, Mike Broome,
Anthony Brockhouse; UK: Ginnie Pepper

Norway, 1970

Roger Chapman, Patrick Brook, Geoff Holder, Peter Booth, Brendan
O'Brien, Bob Powell, Henrik Forss, David Murray-Wells, Vanda Allfrey,
Rosemary Alhusen, Jane Moncreiff, Johnnie Muir, Gillie Kennard;
UK: George Greenfield

Canada, 1971

Jack McConnell, Joe Skibinski, Stanley Cribbett, Ginnie Fiennes,
Sarah Salt, Bryn Campbell, Ben Usher, Richard Robinson, Paul Berriff,
Wally Wallace; UK: Mike Gannon, Spencer Eade

Greenland/North Pole, 1976–78

Oliver Shepard, Charlie Burton, Ginnie Fiennes, Geoff Newman,
Mary Gibbs; UK: Mike Wingate Gray, Andrew Croft, Peter Booth

Transglobe, 1979–82

Oliver Shepard, Charlie Burton, Ginnie Fiennes, Simon Grimes,
Anton Bowring, Les Davis, Ken Cameron, Cyrus Balapoira, Howard
Willson, Mark Williams, Dave Hicks, Dave Peck, Jill McNicol, Ed Pike,
Paul Anderson, Terry Kenchington, Martin Weymouth, Annie Weymouth,
Jim Young, Geoff Lee, Nigel Cox, Paul Clark, Admiral Otto Steiner,
Mick Hart, Commander Ramsey, Nick Wade, Anthony Birkbeck,
Giles Kershaw, Gerry Nicholson, Karl Z'berg, Chris McQuaid,
Lesley Rickett, Laurence Howell, Edwyn Martin, John Parsloe, Peter Polley
and others; UK: Anthony Preston, David Mason, Janet Cox, Sue Klugman,